American Idols
Overcoming the False Gods that Keep Us from Abundant Life

Jeff Berger

Cover art by Kayleigh Berger

OTHER BOOKS BY JEFF BERGER:

Available on Amazon or by contacting the author:

Hark the Herald Angels Sing: A Christmas Devotional, 2015

Finding Jesus, 2019

Now You Tell Me: What I Wish I'd Known Before I Got Married, 2020

Contents

Chapter 1

The Sickness in Our Souls

They sit in the Warden's office, discussing the arrival of a prisoner to death row. Paul, the commander of that section of the prison, is dressed in the blue cap and uniform of a prison guard. Hal, the Warden, wears a business suit. They've worked together for many years, and have become friends as well as colleagues. This new prisoner is a problem child, and Hal wants to be sure Paul and his men are ready for him. In the middle of his last sentence, Hal's voice falters. Paul looks up. "Hal?" The Warden looks at his friend. "It's a tumor, Paul. A brain tumor. They got X-ray pictures of it. It's the size of a lemon, they said, and way down deep inside where they can't operate. They say she'll be dead by Christmas. I haven't told her. I can't think how. For the life of me, Paul, I can't think how to tell my wife she's going to die." At this, Hal dissolves into tears. He sobs uncontrollably as Paul looks on, helpless. These are tough men, who regularly see the worst this world has to offer. Yet neither has the resources to confront this terrible event.

That's not a real-life conversation, but a scene from The Green Mile, a movie released in 1999. Later in the film, we meet Melinda, Hal's wife. She is an elegant, churchgoing woman, but Hal confides in Paul that the tumor has changed her personality. She has become angry and profane. Hal says, "I didn't know she'd ever heard those words." By the next time we see her, the awful metamorphosis has changed her appearance, wasting away her body and deforming her facial features. The Green Mile isn't a movie about Hal and Melinda; they are minor characters in the story. But they stand out in my memory because of that scene in Hal's office. As a pastor, I've had similar conversations with husbands and wives, parents and children. Though there is a lot about that movie that is obviously fictional (it's about a death row prisoner with healing powers, after all), that scene

1

rings true. I recognize the struggle to understand. How can someone who looks perfectly healthy have inside them ("way down deep inside where they can't operate") a spreading malignancy that will kill them slowly, painfully, relentlessly?

This is a book about something even more dangerous than cancer. Idolatry is a spiritual sickness that, like Melinda's brain tumor, takes root in our minds and hearts, warping our character, leaching away our joy, our peace, and our capacity to love others. Its end is death...not a death of the body, but of the soul. It's terrifying to consider: We can build what seems like the perfect life. Meanwhile, this disease is there, way down deep inside, slowly destroying its host--us. The good news is that, unlike physical cancer, there is a sure-fire cure. That's also what this book is about: The path to overcoming what I believe to be the main thing standing between us and what Jesus called "life more abundant."

I am blessed to live near the world's preeminent cancer treatment center, MD Anderson Hospital in Houston. In 1996, Irve Le Moyne, a rear admiral in the US Navy, completed his treatment for head and neck cancer at Anderson. He brought a large brass bell to his last treatment, explaining to his nurses and doctor that the Navy had a tradition of ringing a bell to signify "when the job was done." Admiral Le Moyne rang his bell that day, and left it as a donation for others to use. I have been in Anderson Hospital on more than one occasion when the bell was rung, and the sense of joy is palpable. That tradition has now spread to hospitals across our country. There is something wonderful about beating the unseen enemy, knowing that you can finally, fully experience life as it was meant to be. I hope that this book will be used of God to bring that sort of joyous freedom and victory in your life.

Defining Idolatry

If you're like most Christians, you think of idol worship as a relic from the Old Testament. We recall the first two of the Ten Commandments: You shall have no other gods before me, and You shall not make for yourself a carved image (Exodus 20:3-4. All Scripture references are from the English Standard Version, unless

2

otherwise noted). Idolatry, it seems, is worshipping and serving anything other than God Himself. But you don't see how such a subject could be relevant to you. "After all," you muse, "I've never bowed down to a statue or prayed to the sun. I don't even check my horoscope." With all due respect, I think you're wrong. I think you and I and every other follower of Christ has at least one false god lurking in our subconscious, calling seductively for our true allegiance. I believe idolatry is at least as prevalent and damaging in 21st Century American Christianity as it was in Israel three thousand years ago. In fact, I think our idolatry is the main reason for the decline of the American Church's vibrancy and cultural impact over the past fifty years. So how do I define idolatry?

While the idols mentioned in Scripture were often physical objects--man-made statues representing other gods, or natural objects that were worshipped as if they were personal beings—the Bible also makes it clear that non-physical things can be idols:

• In 1 Samuel 15:23, the prophet Samuel tells King Saul, *presumption is as iniquity and idolatry.* Saul had started out as a humble ruler, but now he was acting like the kings of other nations, setting up monuments to himself and keeping the spoils of war rather than sacrificing them, as God commanded. In Samuel's view, Saul's lust for political power had become his true god.

• In Jeremiah 2 and 3, the prophet criticizes Israel's kings for making treaties with godless nations, instead of relying on God's protection. They have no faith in God, Jeremiah says, because they worship security instead.

• In Ezekiel 14:3, God tells Ezekiel that the elders of Israel have taken their idols into their hearts. They aren't bowing before statues, but their hearts have elevated something else above the Lord Himself.

• Habakkuk 1:11 calls the enemies of God's people guilty, because their own strength is their god.

• Paul in both Ephesians 5:5 and Colossians 3:5 refers to greed as idolatry.

Note what God is saying to us: Idols aren't necessarily entities that are recognized as gods in any religious sense. They aren't necessarily things we can see or touch. An idol can be literally anything, even a very good thing, like the desire to be safe, or the ambition to be successful...or even the person you love most in the world. Martin Luther defined idolatry as "anything on which your heart relies or depends." Your true god is whatever is ultimate in your life. It's what you base your security, identity, and purpose upon. It's what people think of when they think of you. It's anything you cannot imagine living without. Whatever is your true god determines your choices, shapes your character, and defines your life.

In 2005, the brilliant novelist David Foster Wallace was invited to deliver the commencement address at Kenyon College. His comments have been widely quoted ever since, especially this section:

"Because here's something else that's weird but true: in the day-to day trenches of adult life, there is actually no such thing as atheism. There is no such thing as not worshipping. Everybody worships. The only choice we get is what to worship. And the compelling reason for maybe choosing some sort of god or spiritual-type thing to worship— be it JC or Allah, be it YHWH or the Wiccan Mother Goddess, or the Four Noble Truths, or some inviolable set of ethical principles—is that pretty much anything else you worship will eat you alive. If you worship money and things, if they are where you tap real meaning in life, then you will never have enough, never feel you have enough. It's the truth. Worship your body and beauty and sexual allure and you will always feel ugly. And when time and age start showing, you will die a million deaths before they finally grieve you. On one level, we all know this stuff already. It's been codified as myths, proverbs, clichés, epigrams, parables; the skeleton of every great story. The whole trick is keeping the truth up front in daily consciousness."

Wallace was not a religious man in any conventional sense (as you can probably tell by the reference to "JC or Allah...YHWH or the Wiccan Mother Goddess"). Yet he recognized that we are all made to worship something. He went on to say that this wasn't a conscious choice, but a "default setting" in our hearts. We slip into the worship of unseen gods without even knowing it. As John Calvin famously wrote, the heart is an idol factory. Wallace recognized, also, that idolatry is nurtured by the culture we live in: "And the world will not discourage you from operating on your default-settings, because the world of men and money and power hums along quite nicely on the fuel of fear and contempt and frustration and craving and the worship of self." His message can be summed up in this sentence: We all worship something, and if we worship the wrong thing, it will destroy us. It's a message the biblical prophets would have said a hearty "amen" to. You may never have noticed how deeply the narrative of Scripture is really the story of God's mission to rescue us from our idols. Let me show you what I mean.

A Quick Bible Tour

The story of idolatry in the human race goes back much further than Moses coming down from Mt Sinai with the Ten Commandments. It's the story of humanity's fall. Genesis 3 tells us the first human sin—which brought pain, sickness, violence and death into the world—was motivated by a desire to "be like God" (Genesis 3:5). Adam and Eve had a perfect world, but it wasn't enough for them. They wanted equal status with the Lord Himself. They displaced the Almighty as King of their hearts, and put themselves in His place. Their own desire to call the shots became their true god, and the Lord allowed them to follow that god to their heart's content...and to their ultimate misery.

Humanity didn't learn from that first, critical mistake. By the time God first appeared to Abraham in Genesis 12, the earth was full of counterfeit gods. Men and women, in an attempt to find security and happiness in an uncertain world, had enslaved themselves to a multiplicity of cruel deities. Is it time for harvest? You'd better offer a sacrifice to the God of fertility. Are you experiencing a drought? Visit a priest of the storm god, but be sure to bring an offering. Building a house? All sorts of things could go wrong, so a prudent man sacrifices a child to appease the unseen host of belligerent spirits who are ready to pounce upon him. Abraham was seventy-five and financially well off, living in the land of Ur. Serving these fickle gods seemed to be working out better for him than for most. But God told him there was another, better way, and he would be the beginning of a new race of people. Abraham and Sarah's descendants would bless the entire world by showing them there was only One God, and that real life was found in following Him alone.

Exodus is well-known as the story of God freeing His people from slavery, but the Lord had another motive as well: In Exodus 12:12, He told Moses He was also executing judgment on the gods of Egypt. The Egyptians, like most people in those days, had gods and goddesses who they trusted to control every aspect of their lives. When the Lord brought His ten plagues upon their land, each plague was a direct assault on the power of one or more of those gods. For example, when Moses changed the water of the Nile to blood, it proved that the Egyptian god of the Nile, Hapi, was powerless. When Egypt's crops were destroyed, Osiris the god of fertility was nowhere to be found. And when the sky grew dark for three consecutive days, Ra the sun god, most revered of all the Egyptian deities, was exposed as a fraud. Some Egyptians got the message. In Exodus 9, when Moses predicted a catastrophic hailstorm, some of the people of the land rushed to bring their workers and animals inside to protect them. They were spared, while those who trusted in the storm god, Set, watched helplessly as their livestock perished. In the end, some Egyptians left along with the Israelites on their Exodus (Ex. 12:38). They were now convinced that the Lord alone was God.

Perhaps in moments of weakness and doubt, you've thought to yourself, "I wish God would prove Himself to me. Speak out loud, or even do something as simple as make my bedroom light flicker. If I could just see a miracle—just one!—I would believe and never doubt again." If you've ever thought this way, you need to pay attention to what happened to the Israelites a few weeks after their miraculous deliverance from slavery (Exodus 32). Keep in mind, these people had just witnessed, over the course of several months, the total devastation of the people who had murdered their children and enslaved them for generations. Everything God had said to them through Moses had come true. Then they had walked through a parted Sea on ground that was unexplainably dry, and seen their enemies drowned to death behind them. Now they traveled each day with visible evidence of God guiding them through the desert, in the form of a pillar of cloud by day and a pillar of fire by night. They ate bread that materialized every night while they slept, and drank water that flowed from rocks.

Yet the first time their spiritual leader Moses left them (when he went atop Mt Sinai for forty days to receive the Law), they immediately lost faith. With the active participation of Aaron their High Priest, they made a calf out of gold and said, "Here's our god, who rescued us from Egypt!" How could they do such a foolish thing? Our fickle hearts prefer gods we can control and comprehend. The Lord Almighty is beyond our understanding. We can't wrap our minds around His thoughts and plans. We simply have to follow Him and wait to see where He's taking us. For a lot of us, that leap of faith is a bridge too far.

A second reason Israel turned to a golden calf is that the One True God expects us to be holy people. He holds us accountable for the way we treat our neighbors, especially those who are lower than we are on the social ladder. He cares who we sleep with, how we spend our money, the way we speak, the thoughts we indulge. In contrast, a god of our own making has no such expectations. We know the score with our man-made gods. We can shape them into our own image, and live the life we've always wanted. Even better, we can do that while simultaneously telling ourselves, "I'm still worshipping God." Every time we read the story of the golden calf, we need to remember: We make the same ridiculous mistake, time and again.

The rest of the history of Old Testament Israel (as seen in the books of Judges, Samuel, Kings and Chronicles) is a frustrating cycle: God's people drift into idolatry. Their new gods fail them, and soon they find themselves conquered and oppressed by other nations. They cry out to God for help, and He sends a deliverer (either a military hero like one of the Judges—Gideon, Deborah, Samson—or a good king like David, Hezekiah, or Josiah). The people are rescued, and they return to wholehearted devotion to the God who loves them. For a time, there is prosperity, but then they start to drift again. We rinse and repeat.

One important thing to note: In many of these stories, the Israelites don't abandon God entirely. They continue to observe many aspects of the Law, offer their sacrifices in the Tabernacle or Temple, and keep the festivals. It's just that they add in these other gods as well. It seems to have been common for an otherwise devout Israelite to have small statues of foreign gods in his home, or to visit "high places" where sacrifices could be offered to the gods of other nations. It was a way of hedging one's bets: "Sure, I believe in Yahweh. Why wouldn't I, after all He's done for our people? But this next harvest is critical, so I also sacrifice to Baal. And I have an Asherah pole outside my house, because my Canaanite neighbors who worship her seem to be doing pretty well for themselves." Again, this is a lesson for us: We can be morally upright and doctrinally sound in our beliefs, and still be guilty of idolatry. If we trust in anything other than Him to bring us safety, happiness, significance, that thing is our true object of worship.

The idolatry of the Israelites was their downfall. God eventually said, "If you want these other gods, I will let you have them. See where they take you. Then perhaps you'll return to me and be saved." Their new gods led Israel to disaster, invasion, and exile to a foreign land. Around 600 BC, the temple in Jerusalem was destroyed, and thousands of people were carried away to Babylon, never to see the Promised Land again.

They couldn't say they weren't warned. In the years leading up to this calamitous event, God had sent prophet after prophet to diagnose the people's problem, and to tell them exactly what would happen if they didn't root the cancer of idolatry out of their hearts. Men like Isaiah and Amos saw it coming from a distance. Others like Jeremiah and Ezekiel lived through it, and helped the people understand what had gone wrong. I have to admit, I don't enjoy the prophetic books. Those men seem so angry and humorless. But there's a reason for that. They are like parents watching their own children destroy themselves. A mother or father whose kids have gone off the rails will go to any lengths to get their attention, and that's what the prophets did. They shouted. They threatened. They humiliated themselves with shocking acts of symbolism, like Isaiah stripping naked, or Ezekiel refusing to mourn when his beloved wife died. They used shocking language, too. Often, they compared the behavior of Israel to a wandering spouse. Sometimes, they spoke of this spiritual adultery in terms we find disturbingly graphic even in our R-rated culture. Hosea took it to the ultimate extent: He actually married a prostitute, Gomer, then wept as she left him and their children to return to her old ways. When the people saw a holy man make such a decision, it should have gotten their attention. It should have made them see that they were the prostitutes, spitting in the face of the God who had saved them time and again, and choosing a life that led to degradation and death. But they still wouldn't listen.

Hosea ended up ransoming his faithless wife, purchasing her from her pimp and loving her as if she had been faithful all along. God, too, refused to abandon His philandering people. Against all the odds, the Jews were set free. They returned to the Promised Land and rebuilt the temple. Better still, they seemed to have finally learned their lesson. After the exile, Israel never again worshipped the gods of other nations. Now that they had no king, ordinary citizens took it upon themselves to police the nation, keeping everyone faithful to the Law of Moses.

By the time Jesus arrived these men, the scribes and Pharisees, were revered by the people for keeping them from the tragic errors of the past. Yet Jesus pointed out a terrible irony: These same men were leading the people into idolatry of another form. We'll explore this idea in more detail in chapter 8, but the religious leaders of Israel worshipped their own religious traditions and self-written moral codes. Their devotion to their own version of holiness was so complete, when God Himself visited them in human form, they didn't even recognize Him. When He challenged them to abandon their idols and return to the Way, the Truth and the Life, it angered them so deeply they wanted Him dead.

The Bible ends with John the Apostle's spectacular vision. Far too many self-important preachers have misused the book of Revelation to scare the pants off of people (and make themselves rich and famous). I don't claim to know what every scroll, bowl, trumpet and creature represents. But here's what I see: People worshipping a beast, a false prophet, and a glorious, bustling city (Revelation 13, 17-18) instead of God. In my opinion, this represents our tendency to chase after military/political power and the leaders who offer it (the beast), man-made religious movements (the false prophet), and the world's version of wealth and success (the city of Babylon). No matter how you interpret Revelation, the story of Scripture starts with humans replacing the Lord with gods of their own desires, and ends with Jesus destroying all our idols and reigning over us forever as everlasting, righteous and loving King.

The Solution

If idol-worship is our default setting, what can we do about it? As I said at the beginning, this is a book of hope. My prayer is that it leads to personal renewal for all those who read it. But my prayers are actually even greater than that. All my life, I have heard preachers call for revival in our nation. In the past few years, I have come to understand what that would look like if (and prayerfully, when) it happens. The revival of the American Church would look like Christians exposing their own idols, and putting Jesus back on the throne of their hearts, families, and churches. When Jesus is truly our Savior and King, instead of the figurehead we claim to worship while actually pursuing other things, we will live with purpose, peace, and joy. We will build healthy families and authentic friendships. We will love non-Christians in a shockingly counter-cultural way; it will be the kind of love that speaks louder than political disputes or religious arguments. We will, in other words, finally and fully be the people Jesus had in mind when He said:

You are the light of the world. A city set on a hill cannot be hidden. Nor do people light a lamp and put it under a basket, but on a stand, and it gives light to all in the house. In the same way, let your light shine before others, that they may see your good works, and give glory to your Father who is in Heaven. (Matthew 5:14-16)

No, I don't think this little book is going to make that happen. Only the Holy Spirit can do something that amazing…and I hope you're praying for it, every day. But if this book changes your life in some small way; if you allow my words to expose a rival god in your heart and put that interloper in its place, ushering Jesus back into His rightful spot as unquestioned King, it will have been worth it. So how do we accomplish that? In my opinion, there are two things that must happen.

First, we must identify our idols. This is the tricky part. When my daughter was a little girl (about three) she got a splinter in her hand, right in the meaty part of her palm. My wife knew that tiny shard of wood had to come out, but Kayleigh refused to let her mom touch that hand. This went on for days. Finally, her little palm was bright red, and she was walking with her hand pressed against her tummy, it was hurting so bad. Carrie said, "We've got to do something, whether she wants us to or not." And by "something" she meant I had to hold my daughter completely still while my wife used a needle to dig that thing out of her hand. That was tough. Even though she was a tiny thing, only about thirty pounds, and I thought I was a pretty strong guy, it was taking all I had to keep her still. Part of the problem was that I had to be careful not to crush her with my weight while she struggled. She screamed and cried and made the most heartbreaking noises. It seemed to take forever. When we were done, all three of us were in tears. But it was worth it. Once that splinter was out, her hand healed up, and everything was fine.

Identifying our idols will be something like that. Few of us are willing to admit that we are, at heart, idol worshippers. And your idols, whatever they may be, are embedded so deeply in your heart, you will resist any effort to expose them. You'll even get angry if someone confronts you about an idol. I'm telling you right now, most of you will want to throw this book across the room at some point or another. A threat to your idol will feel like a personal insult, and a deathly threat to your way of life. All I am asking is that you read the coming chapters with an open mind and a prayerful, humble heart. Our next chapter will be about how to identify the idols in your life. Each of the following chapters will focus on one specific form of idolatry that I see as especially influential in American culture—and in American Christianity—today. I hope you will begin to see, as I do, the idolatry that has infected the Church today. More importantly, I hope you are able to be honest with yourself about the idols that lurk in your heart, jockeying for your allegiance. Please understand, I don't claim any authority on this subject, aside from the authority of God's Word. Check my words against the Bible. If you find that my thoughts aren't Scriptural, burn this book with my blessing. But if God's Spirit highlights an area of inconsistency in your life, please…for the love of all that is holy (literally) don't ignore His still, small voice.

I had a friend years ago who was about my age (mid-thirties at that time). One day, he told me that he was worried about his health. He was suffering from fairly intense abdominal pain, as well as other related symptoms. I had gone through something similar a few years before, but with the help of a gastroenterologist, I had recovered. I urged him to follow up on this, giving him my doctor's name and contact information. He thanked me, but never went. When I pressed him about why, he said that he was afraid of what the doctor might find. For him, not knowing seemed better than uncovering the truth. I argued that he should go for the sake of his wife and small child, since there was a chance that even a dire issue was more likely to be treatable if they diagnosed it early. But he was unconvinced. A few years later, we moved away, and I lost contact with him. Hopefully, whatever he was struggling with resolved itself. But here's my point: You may feel like he did about the idolatries in your own life. You may resist thinking too deeply about this issue, because you're afraid of what it might lead to: "What if God makes me give up something I really enjoy?" I urge you not to make that mistake. For your own sake, and for those who love you, let God show you the idols that must be confronted. And then take action.

What kind of action? That's the second thing we must do: Bring our idols to Jesus. The first Christians gave up so much to follow Him. Peter and Andrew, James and John walked away from the family business. Matthew left behind a cushy position as a tax collector. Mary Magdalene and several other women financed the Lord's work out of their own pockets. And Saul of Tarsus traded his prominent position as a religious leader for the lowly state of a virtual fugitive from the people who once revered him. They gave everything to Jesus, even the things most precious to them, and they never regretted that decision. In each chapter, I will outline specific ways we can bring those idols to Jesus. And I'll end the book with a glimpse of what it would take to live forever free from idolatry.

In The Green Mile, Paul the prison guard decides he must try to save Melinda, his friend's wife (If you've never seen the movie and don't want it spoiled, skip this paragraph). There is a prisoner Paul oversees on death row named John Coffey, who is unusual in many ways. Convicted of killing two little girls, Coffey is a towering, muscular behemoth, but seems as gentle as a child. More importantly, he has shown on several occasions an ability to heal people, including Paul himself. Paul convinces his fellow guards to do a dangerous, highly illegal thing: To take John Coffey out of prison in the dead of night, drive him to Hal and Melinda's house, and see if he can heal her. When Coffey encounters Melinda, twisted and deranged by the tumor in her brain, he breathes deeply, absorbing the sickness into himself. Melinda is restored in every way, but now Coffey bears her affliction. Stephen King, the author of the book The Green Mile is based on, is not a Christian, but his character John Coffey is one of my favorite images of Jesus Christ in any movie. For, just like Coffey, our Lord was executed for crimes He did not commit. And just like Coffey, He bore our sins and carried our afflictions. Colossians 2:13-14 says that He took everything that was against us and nailed it to the cross. That includes our idols. So once we identify those idols, we bring them to Jesus. We confess them to Him. He will take them away, so that we can be free.

What does that look like in real-life terms? That's what we'll talk about in the rest of this book. But for now, let me leave you with this thought: You may be worried about questions like, "What if my idol is my job? Do I need to become unemployed? Or what if my idol is my family? Does God want me to leave them?" Jesus knows the answers to those questions. He knows how to put everything in your life into its proper place. He is, after all, the One who found a way to save you and me against all the odds, and He was willing to go to the uttermost lengths to accomplish it. You can trust Him to handle your idols.

Chapter 2:

Identifying Your Idols

I've known I needed to write this book for over a decade. That's when I first realized I had an idolatry problem.

Up until that year, I had an unusually blissful life. I had grown up surrounded by loving, devout Christian people. I had a wife who made me ridiculously happy, two adorable kids who thought I was amazing, and a job I loved. Sure, I had experienced life's ups and downs, but I knew most people would have gladly traded places with me. That year, our little family suffered a series of blows, one after another. Carrie's dad died, followed by my grandfather, who had been a huge influence in my life. Carrie suffered an injury, then went through a painful surgery that turned out to be unsuccessful. Our daughter was entering her teen years, and began pulling away from us emotionally, and away from Christ Himself, which terrified us. Our first-grade son hated his school, and cried every morning when we dropped him off. And while the church I pastored was full of wonderful people, I was experiencing more defeats than victories there as well: We were struggling financially in the wake of the Great Recession. A promising young adult group had vaporized, with each couple leaving our church for various reasons. Whatever the opposite of a "Midas touch" is, I seemed to have it.

One day, I realized the joy had simply vanished from my life. Things that had once captured my heart now held no delight whatsoever. I felt like the best years of my life were gone, and nothing good would happen from now on. To make matters worse, there was no one I could talk to about this. I usually shared everything with Carrie, but I knew I couldn't unload all of this on her. I certainly couldn't tell anyone in my church what I was going through; no church wants a pastor who mopes his way through life. The most troubling thing for me was that my faith in Christ was supposed to bring me joy, regardless of my circumstances. That's what I had been preaching for years. And, until that point, it's what I had experienced, as well. No matter what life threw at me, I found peace and hope in my relationship with God. Why wasn't that working now?

Then I remembered something I'd heard in a seminary class a few years before. It was a class on preaching, but on this day, Dr. Al Fasol steered our discussion in another direction. He told us about the mid-life crisis he had endured years before, and essentially said, "Watch out, boys. It's coming for you, too." When most people hear the term "mid-life crisis" they picture a man in his forties getting an ear pierced, buying a convertible, and flirting with women half his age. But Dr. Fasol told us to ignore that cliché. Instead, he described it as a general sense of worthlessness. A man in those years will feel he has missed the mark in every aspect of his life. He urged us to be ready for those middle years, to deepen our walk with Christ in preparation. He said, "Stick close to the Lord. You'll need Him then like you've never needed Him before." I remember thinking it would never happen to me. I loved life, and didn't expect that to ever change. Yet here I was, experiencing everything Dr. Fasol had warned us about. But that wasn't my only surprise.

As I prayed and sought answers in God's Word, I made a startling realization: My sorrow was the result of my idols being displaced. I idolized my marriage, but with Carrie and me each struggling with our own separate issues, we experienced conflict and emotional distance like I didn't think possible. I idolized feeling like a "super dad," but I now felt powerless to fix the increasingly complex problems my kids were going through as they grew up. I idolized being young and vibrant, but now I saw that would slip away in the not-too-distant future. I idolized being a successful pastor, but at that point in my life, I felt like a failure. Before that year, I would have said I was fully committed to Christ. But now, in light of the despair I felt when those parts of my life were threatened (not lost, mind you, only threatened), I saw clearly the staggering truth: I was an idol worshipper. As I look back on that difficult period of my life, I am immensely grateful for how God used that time to wean me from these idolatries. I am a much better husband, father, pastor and most of all, disciple of Jesus than I would have been if everything had gone my way.

So...just ask God to give you a series of personal tragedies and disappointments, followed by a season of deep malaise, and you'll identify your idols in no time!

Thankfully, that's NOT the message of this chapter. Actually, I'd like to spare you the pain of going through what I experienced, if possible. I'd like to help you identify your idols and put them in their proper place in your life. Here's why:

What Idols Do to Us

The second commandment says *You shall not make for yourself a carved image...You shall not bow down to them or serve them, for I the Lord your God am a jealous God* (Ex 20:4-5). Let's be honest: this bothers us. We can't understand how God can be so exclusive. How can He say, "I am jealous," as if that's a good thing? We hear the word "jealous" and think of a possessive teenaged boy who tries to control every aspect of his girlfriend's life, who gets violently angry when he sees her talking to another boy, or threatens to kill himself if she breaks up with him. We all agree that's not love; it's selfishness. But there is such a thing as righteous jealousy. When jealousy comes from a place of self-sacrificial love for that person, it is a good thing. It's a jealousy that says, "I will defend you from those who want to harm you. I will speak hard words of truth to you when you're headed in a self-destructive direction. I will not stand idly by while your life is ruined." Anyone who grew up in a healthy home has experienced this sort of jealousy. Good parents are jealous for the health, safety and flourishing of their children. Sometimes this means advocating for their kids when they aren't receiving the help they need from the medical industry or the school system. Other times, it means protecting them from bullies (or possessive boyfriends). And still other times, it means confronting and disciplining the kids themselves to keep them from forming damaging habits.

Perhaps an even better analogy is a man who falls in love with a woman who is recovering from a devastating addiction to drugs. He marries her, and together they build a beautiful new life. One day, he sees a text message on her phone from the man who was once her drug dealer. He asks, "What is he doing contacting you?" She says, "He just got out of jail. We're going to have a big reunion, me and all my old friends, at his new apartment." Is that husband justified in being upset? Should he plead with his wife not to go, to remember how miserable her life was before and not take any chances on going back? Of course. In fact, I couldn't fault him if he calls this man up and says, "Stay away from my wife. I'll gladly go to jail for assault or murder rather than let my wife go back to where she was before." Yet God loves us infinitely more than any husband ever loved his wife, and infinitely more than any parent loved her child. He is jealous for us because He knows what our idols do to us. Let's talk about that. Why are idols so dangerous?

Our idols change us. Psalm 115 is about the stupidity of idol worship. It says idols can't see, hear, smell, walk or talk. Why would anyone worship a "god" who is powerless to help them? Then in verse 8 it says, Those who make them become like them; so do all who trust in them. Bible scholar GK Beale wrote a book based on that verse called We Become What We Worship. He points out that after the Israelites in Egypt create a golden calf to worship (Exodus 32), God starts calling them "a stiff-necked people." Stiff-necked means "hard to lead."

Several years ago, I was helping my dad with his cattle. We were trying to separate the calves from the cows, so we could take them to market. One big bull calf wasn't having it. He was about five hundred pounds, and stubborn, and we couldn't get him through the gate. I chased that bull back and forth, whacking him with my stick, trying to turn him toward that gate. Suddenly, he turned toward me, ducked his head and charged. When I planted my foot to jump out of the way, my boots sank into the mud and manure of that cow pen, and I fell over backwards. The young bull ran right over me. I got up, feeling an intense pain from where his hooves had scraped across my chest, but otherwise glad to still be alive. Eventually, Dad and I got him into the pen, but then we couldn't get him into the trailer. At one point, he turned and rammed his (thankfully, hornless) head into my thigh, pinning me to the side of the fence. For the next month, I would be a walking contusion, my chest changing from yellow to purple to black, and the bone bruise in my thigh causing me to limp like an arthritic senior citizen. Eventually, with the help of my brother (who got off work just in time to come to the rescue), we loaded the infernal beast and took him and the other calves to the market. My dad was awfully glad to get that over with—and felt a little sorry for me--so he offered to buy me anything I wanted for supper. We went to Whataburger. I got a double. I enjoyed every bite.

The theme of Beale's book is this sentence: "What people revere, they resemble, whether for ruin or restoration." If we worship God and Him alone, we will begin to take on His character. We will love others like He does. We will develop courage, humility, mercy and wisdom. But worshipping anything else will change us to our ruin. The people of God had just started worshipping this calf, and they had already become like him, so stiff-necked they were more likely to fight God than follow Him. How have your idols changed you? If you worship money, you'll live in constant anxiety over the fluctuations of the stock market. If you worship success, you won't have any true friendships; just people you use to get further ahead. If you worship comfort, it makes you lazy and fearful. Here's one sure way to know when something has become an idol: Imagine what it would be like if that thing were suddenly removed from your life. If you think life wouldn't be worth living in that case, you've identified an idol. You've adapted your identity to the thing you worship, and you can't imagine happiness without it.

Our idols consume us. Many scholars have noted the link between idolatry and addiction; in both cases, we turn to something other than God to be our "refuge and strength," our "very present help in trouble." We certainly see that in the vicious cycle that Israel went through. Idolatry consumes us so completely, we won't listen to reason. We become unreasonably angry if anyone threatens it. In Exodus 32, when Moses saw what the Israelites had done, he smashed the newly-carved tablets of the Ten Commandments to the ground in disgust. But this didn't stop the drunken revelry of the Israelites. They were so out of control, Moses asked for his fellow men from the tribe of Levi to put a stop to it, and they ended up killing three thousand of their fellow Israelites before order was restored.

In Acts 19, we see a riot break out in the city of Ephesus

because the preaching of the Gospel was drawing people away from the worship of the goddess Artemis. Her temple was a source of revenue for the city, and some of the people who worked near there started the riot, because they thought their livelihoods were being threatened by this new religion...after all, more converts to Christ means fewer potential worshippers of Artemis. They dragged several Christians into an arena, threatening to kill them, and chanted "Great is Artemis of the Ephesians!" for two solid hours. These were civilized people, but they completely lost their minds because their idol was threatened.

Think about the last few times you've lost your temper. If you're honest with yourself, you can probably trace that anger to some form of idolatry. Your friends tell you what that vile woman in your office is saying about you, and you can't wait to make her pay. Why? You know it's not true, so why does it bother you? Because other people in the office will believe it. Your reputation is more important to you than that woman's soul...more important, in fact, than the command of God to love our enemies. Your wife complains that you're not at home enough, and you fly into a rage. You should be glad she wants you around more; why does this make you mad? Because she wants you to spend less time at work, or on the golf course, the lake, or the hunting lease. None of these things are evil, mind you. But they are obviously more important to you than your relationship with your wife...and more important than God's command to love her as Christ loved us, laying down His life for us (Ephesians 5:25). Your parents take away your cell phone and you explode. You threaten, you cry, you scream, "I hate you!" Why? Your anger is a clue to your idolatry, because this device—intended to be a tool for your convenience—has instead become your master. It has consumed your life. That is what idols do.

Our idols drive people away from God. You may wonder, "Why would the Israelites want to worship a golden calf?" Archaeologists have discovered that a calf was a common object of worship in that part of the world, including in Egypt. In other words, the Israelites had seen other people worshipping golden calves and said, "Let's get what they have." There are many things we could say about that decision, but here's one: God had just given His people the

Law. The whole purpose of the Law was so that they would be His treasured possession, His Kingdom of Priests, His Holy Nation (Exodus 19:5-6). They were supposed to be different from all other peoples on earth. They were the ones who would show the world that strength was found in taking care of the poor, orphans, widows, and immigrants. They would be the first country that required men to be faithful to their wives. They would take off work one day a week in honor of their God, and somehow be even more productive than the rest of the world that worked non-stop. Best of all, they would worship one God, a God who was loving and righteous, instead of living in constant fear of dozens of gods who would smite you if you didn't keep up with the constant sacrifices to their images. As they lived out this Law, other nations would see the joy that came from following their God, and would come to them for salvation. But the moment Israel cast that golden calf, they chose to forfeit their purpose. They wanted to be like everyone else.

Our idols do the same to us. As Christians, we too are called to be God's royal priests, and holy people (1 Peter 2:9). We're called to be the light of the world, the salt of the earth, and a city on a hill (Matthew 5:13-16). Our purpose is to stand out from our neighbors in such a compelling, inviting way that they want what we have. Or as Dallas Willard once put it: "To glorify God means...to live in such a way that when people see us they think, Thank God for God, if God would create such a life."

But idolatry makes us forfeit that purpose. Instead of standing out, we lust for the things our neighbors have. We even convince ourselves that God's job is to get us those things. Then we have the nerve to wonder why people have stopped coming to our churches, and why the Gospel isn't spreading as it once was in America. Let's look at this realistically: Why would our neighbors be drawn to what we have, when all they can see is that we worship money, sex, power, politics, success, approval, and comfort, just like they do, only we put a religious veneer on it? It's idolatry with a side of hypocrisy...not a very inviting combo meal. We won't fulfill our purpose until we put our idols in their proper place.

Our idols disappoint us. CJH Wright says, "We tend to

idolize the things (or people, or systems) that we place our trust in to deliver us from the things we fear." If you fear being poor, you'll worship money. If you fear being alone, you'll worship marriage and family. If you fear getting old and unattractive, you'll worship fitness and beauty. The problem with all of those things is that they eventually disappoint you. Wright goes on to say, "Ultimately, it seems, we never learn that false gods never fail to fail. That is the only thing about a false god you can depend on." Your money goes away, no matter how smart you are, or you die and leave it to your ungrateful heirs, who waste it all. Your kids grow up and move out of the house one day, and you're devastated. If you expect your marriage to fulfill you, you will end up crushing your spouse under the weight of your expectations. And no matter how much you exercise, no matter how much moisturizer you apply, Father Time is still undefeated.

In Exodus 32, the Israelites were terrified of uncertainty. They wanted a god they could see and control, who would do whatever they wanted him to, not the God who had saved them, whose ways and thoughts were hard to understand. So they built a custom-made golden god. The results were disastrous. In the end, out of hundreds of thousands of people who were liberated from slavery by the Lord, only two made it to the Promised Land. Only two members of that generation—Joshua and Caleb—experienced the fulness of the salvation God had planned for them.

Many Christians wonder why the life promised them in the Bible doesn't seem to be panning out. They read about "life more abundant" and "my cup runs over," and wonder why they are so unhappy. To be clear, God never promises us a trouble-free life. There will be times—even for the most devoted disciple—when we experience sorrow, stress, trauma, and tragedy (Just read Paul's "resume" in 2 Corinthians 11, if you don't believe me). But the "default setting" of our lives should be joy, peace, and hope.

In my opinion, one of the reasons many of us are disappointed in spite of believing all the correct doctrines and performing all the right rituals is that we're actually trusting in something other than God as our source of identity, security, and happiness. We tell ourselves we are committed followers of Jesus, but what that actually means is, "I believe that if I trust in Jesus, He will ensure that I have a happy marriage, a thriving family, a successful career." Our true god is our marriage, our kids, or our work. We expect the Lord to cooperate with us in feeding that true god. No wonder we're disappointed. Until we begin praying consistently, "Lord, you are all I need. Help me to worship you and you alone," we will keep falling short of the Promised Land.

Diagnosing Idolatry

In the remaining chapters of this book, we'll look closely at the most common idolatries I see in American Christianity today. But virtually anything can be an idol. How can we tell when something (or someone) has become our true god? I suggest we start by asking ourselves the following five questions.

1. What do others think of when they think of me? If you ask any avid baseball fan what they think of when they hear the name, "Ted Williams," they will likely answer: "Hitting." That's exactly the way Williams wanted it. In the summer of 1941, Williams told Pittsburgh Post-Gazette Reporter George Kirksey, "I'd like to break every hitting record in the books. When I walk down the street, I'd like for them to say, 'There goes Ted Williams, the best hitter in baseball." The numbers indicate he accomplished his goal. Williams hit .406 that summer, the last man to bat over .400. He finished his great career with the highest lifetime batting average of the live-ball era. And though his career homerun total places him 20th all-time, most experts believe that if he hadn't missed nearly five full seasons because of military service in World War II and Korea, he would easily hold the record in that category as well. Yet Williams didn't seem to care about other aspects of the game, like defense or baserunning. His frequent clashes with fans and the media were also a distraction. Perhaps as a result, Williams' Red Sox never won a World Series in his nineteen seasons. He idolized hitting, but it didn't bring him inner peace, nor did it help his team reach their goals.

What would your close friends, family, and co-workers say if I mentioned your name? "She's a hard worker." "He sure loves his cars." "You'd better stay on her good side." Their answers could point to our idols, such as our career, our hobby, or our need to get our own way. Even a statement like, "He's the nicest guy I know" might be an indication that your desire to be liked is the thing that motivates you above all. Consider asking those closest to you what they think of when they think of you…if you dare.

2. What do I spend my money on? A man lay dying. His adult son stood over him, weeping. "Dad," he said, "I really wish my kids would have been able to know you." "Show them my checkbook register," the father said, "That will tell them what I was all about." Frankly, I have no proof that story is true. It's a sermon illustration that preachers have been using since approximately the Middle Ages. But it's worth asking yourself, "If someone saw my credit card receipts and bank statements, what would they conclude about my character?"

Not only can money show us where our idols are, it can (ironically) be a way to free us from them. Jesus said in Matthew 6:21, *Where your treasure is, there your heart will be also.* Our hearts tend to follow our money. We know this is true: A young adult who works and saves to buy her own car is much more likely to take care of it than one who is given a car by someone else. A man who invests his money in a tech startup will suddenly find articles about online business trends much more interesting than he did before. If you find yourself wishing you cared more about the things of God, put your money where your good intentions are. Give to world missions, and you will find yourself praying for the work of God in nations you've never visited. Look for opportunities to be generous to people who are struggling, and you'll become more compassionate. Give to the Lord's work, and the Lord's work will become important to you.

3. What inhabits my thoughts and daydreams? Proverbs 4:23 says, *Keep your heart with all vigilance, for from it flow the springs of life.* Colossians 3:2 commands us, *Set your mind on things above, not on things that are on earth.* And Philippians 4:8 tells us, *whatever is true, whatever is honorable, whatever is just, whatever is pure, whatever is lovely, whatever is commendable, if there is any excellence, if there is anything worthy of praise, think about these things.* There's more where those came from, by the way. God is telling us, over and over again, that He cares deeply about our inner lives. We tend to focus on our outer selves, striving for a beautiful, youthful appearance, a well-manicured lawn, a flashy job title, and a carefully curated social media feed. But the true battle for a meaningful, joyful life begins in our minds.

I'm not saying your every conscious thought must be focused on God's glory and helping others. But if the goal of the Christian life is to become like Jesus (and it is) then we should start by trying to think like He does. There are some patterns of thought that are obviously out of bounds: Lustful, pornographic thoughts; indulging in bitter fantasies of revenge; envying the lifestyles of others. But our more innocent thoughts and daydreams can be a clue to identify our idols.

Pay attention today to the things your mind drifts toward in idle moments…while waiting in line at the grocery store, doing chores at home, or trying to fall asleep tonight. There's nothing wrong with imagining what it would be like to live in a nicer neighborhood, or wondering if someone is angry with you, or thinking about who should be the starting safety on your favorite football team. But if those are the things you find yourself thinking of over and over, they are indications that wealth, approval, or your hobbies are too important in your life. It's not just how often you think of certain things; it's what those thoughts produce in you. Taking joy in your ethnic heritage is great, but if it causes you to hate people who are different, it's racism, which is a form of idolatry. Admiring a faithful Christian leader is appropriate, and can lead to growth. But if, when that leader dies or moves on, you stop growing spiritually, or even drop out of church, perhaps you were worshipping the leader more than God. Feeling a deep love for your country is beautiful, and can produce courageous and compassionate actions that are Christianity at its best. But I've attended church services on national holidays in which Jesus and His Word took a backseat to patriotic fanfare. While I love those songs, I left feeling empty; it felt like we were worshipping our country, not Christ.

4. What makes me angry? Oh, how we cherish our anger. Nursing a grudge is as satisfying as a gourmet meal. Posting a rant on social media feels so validating. And when we lose our temper in public, we can't wait to tell everyone we know how justified we were, and how proud we feel for putting that other person in their place. Yet

James 1:20 warns us, *The anger of man does not bring about the righteousness of God.* Proverbs 29:11 says, *A fool gives full vent to his anger, but a wise man holds it in check* (HCSB). And Jesus told us in Matthew 5:22, *But I say to you that everyone who is angry with his brother will be liable to judgment; whoever insults his brother will be liable to the council; and whoever says, 'You fool!' will be liable to the hell of fire.* We quickly point out that Jesus said harsh things about His enemies, and flipped tables in the temple, so clearly it's possible to be angry without sinning. That argument, while true, doesn't usually apply to our anger. Jesus was without sin. His anger was always on behalf of God's glory or the sufferings of others. Every time Jesus was personally insulted, threatened or persecuted, He responded with love, not violence or passive-aggressiveness. Our anger, on the other hand, is almost always a response to our own feelings of being attacked or inconvenienced. It takes a great deal of honesty and humility to recognize the true reasons why we "lose it."

I vividly remember my last fistfight—if it can even be called that. It was before a Little League game, when our coaches had left us alone in the dugout for a few minutes. A boy on my team was complaining loudly to the entire team about the fact that I was starting at second base instead of him. I could feel the heat rising up my neck, turning my face and ears a deep shade of red. Finally, he called me one name too many, and I jumped on him. The resulting tussle wasn't exactly reminiscent of Ali-Frazier. In fact, I don't think either of us even landed a solid punch. Why had I—a fairly easygoing kid—resorted to violence? Because I couldn't allow my peers to think I was weak. Their approval was too important to me. Almost every time I've lost my temper since then, I've been able to see an underlying idolatry behind my anger. What about you? Are you willing to humble yourself and deconstruct the last few times you've done or said something out of anger? Do you dare place your grudges under the microscope of God's Spirit? Pray and ask the Lord to show you the truth about what's really behind your anger.

5. What makes me scared? You may have heard that "fear not" is the most frequently repeated command in the Bible. However, that doesn't mean that it's sinful to feel afraid. On the most basic level, fear is a good thing; it is God's way of keeping us from doing foolish things. When you look at the many times "fear not" is commanded in

Scripture, you see that God isn't judging us for how we feel (which, after all, we can't control), but for what we do in stressful or even terrifying situations. Many of us believe in the common cultural myth that courage is the absence of fear. We see this in movies. I grew up watching John Wayne movies with my dad. I still enjoy many of them—The Searchers, The Quiet Man, and The Man Who Shot Liberty Valance are among my favorite movies of all time. Here's what I see in "The Duke:" He played a variety of characters, including cowboys, outlaws, soldiers, and cops. But he never cried, and he never showed fear. Most of our action stars today follow the same template. Facing an army of foes, with explosions blasting all around them, they wade into the melee without a moment's hesitation. It's all fantasy. In real life, people who behave that way get killed—quickly. Courage isn't the absence of fear; it's being afraid, but doing the right thing anyway. That's what God means when He says, "fear not." He means, "Don't let fear control you. I am the Lord; trust in me, not your fears."

So fear, in and of itself, is not sinful. But our fears are revealing. I'm not talking about our phobias, by the way. The fact that you're terrified of heights, spiders or clowns is not spiritually revealing. I mean whatever causes you persistent, gnawing anxiety, keeps you up at night or causes your stomach to churn is a clue to what is most important in your life. Complete this sentence: "If I lost _____, I don't think I could go on living." What would you put in that blank, if you were totally honest? Is it a person? Your career? A skill that you are proud of? Your appearance? The adulation of a particular group of people? Here's the terrible truth: If any of those things belongs in that blank, you are living a dangerous life. Your life is the equivalent of driving a truck across a bridge made of ice. You hope it'll hold, but sooner or later, you know it's going to fail. It wasn't meant to bear that weight. But if God is in that blank—if He is the One and Only thing that you know you can't live without—then your life is secure. He cannot fail you, He won't leave you, and He will never die. Nothing else in your life can make that guarantee.

We've all lived through times of national tragedy: The explosions of two Space Shuttles, the 9-11 attacks, mass shootings, hurricanes and other natural disasters. Every time, there is a moment of reflection and regret afterwards, in which we collectively say, "This didn't have to happen. The signs were there, clear as day. We just didn't take the time to see them and address them." My fervent prayer is that this book would inspire you to do the hard, humble work of identifying your idols and addressing them, before they do any more damage to your life and witness.

At the start of this chapter, I told you about the moment in my life when I realized what God was doing: He was working, non-stop, to wean me from my idols. That was a tremendous turning point in my life. Now that I know God's primary goal in my life is NOT to give me the life I want, but to make me the man He wants, life makes a great deal more sense. That painstaking process of making me like Jesus, exposing and dethroning my idols along the way, will continue until the day I see Him face-to-face. And if I am wise, I will learn to rejoice in the process, even when it's hard. I will go further than that, in fact. *Forgetting what lies behind and straining forward to what lies ahead, I press on toward the goal for the prize of the upward call of God in Christ Jesus* (Ph. 3:13-14). Now that's a race worth running. Will you join me? Let's take a closer look at some of the idols we need to cast aside.

Chapter 3

Living Large: The Idol of Money and Possessions

A few years ago, I saw an article about happiness. It quoted scientific research that found getting an extra hour of sleep per night makes the average human happier than if that same person made an extra $60,000 a year . My gut-level response was not, "I need to get more sleep." Instead, it was, "If $60,000 isn't enough, I wonder if making an extra $61,000 a year would work?" I thought how much I'd love to be a volunteer in that study. "Give me $61,000? Sure! That's how committed I am to science and human flourishing!" Sadly, none of those eminent researchers—or anyone else—has made that offer to me yet. Come to think of it, that's probably a good thing.

As we've already seen, the Bible explicitly refers to greed as idolatry (Ephesians 5:5, Colossians 3:5). Jesus famously said, *No servant can serve two masters, for either he will hate the one and love the other, or he will be devoted to the one and despise the other. You cannot serve God and money* (Luke 16:13). Where our English Bibles say "money," Jesus used the word "Mammon." That's a word that meant "money, wealth, material possessions," but Jesus personified it. He used it as a personal name. He knew that in the human heart, money and the stuff it buys could easily become a god.

The Seductiveness of Greed

At this point, many of you are probably ready to skip this chapter. You're thinking, "I may have a problem with some form of idolatry, but greed isn't it." But I encourage you to read the chapter anyway. Greed is a sneaky idol. If you struggle with lust, anger, or most other sins, you probably already know it. But most people who worship wealth will never recognize the greed in their hearts. What makes this particular idolatry so hard to see?

Greed is often stereotyped. If you're my age or older, the very word greed conjures up the image of Gordon Gekko, the corporate raider brought to life by Michael Douglas in the 1987 movie Wall Street. Even if you didn't see the movie, you can probably picture him in his Armani suit, with his slicked-back hair, preaching, "Greed is good. Greed works." These days, we're just as likely to see greed embodied in the blinged-out lifestyles of pro athletes, entertainers, and "influencers." Since none of us is a billionaire or an out-of-touch celebrity, we think we're immune to this particular idolatry. But regular people worship mammon, too. And not just those who are "rich" (a relative term, to say the least). Here are some other examples of greed: A woman living in an apartment complex who says, "Once I can afford a house of my own, then I will finally be happy." A man who obsesses over every dollar he makes, and berates his family whenever they spend money in a way he didn't pre-approve. A couple who live like beggars, inside a house crammed floor-to-ceiling with possessions they can't bear to part with. What these people have in common is a desire for more money (or a deep-seated fear of not having enough), that controls their lives and dictates their behavior. A desire for more isn't necessarily a sin. But when that desire controls us, we have a problem.

Greed can seem like "being a good provider." Please understand: If you're struggling financially, it is right for you to want to be able to feed and clothe your family, to provide opportunities for your loved ones to succeed. It's also wise and appropriate to have financial goals, and to work and invest toward them. As a father, I feel an intense inner pressure to make sure my family has what they need. As a husband called to lay down my life for my wife (Eph. 5:25), I ought to be willing to sacrifice whatever is necessary for her to flourish. But there is an unofficial competition among parents that takes our God-given calling as providers and twists it into idolatry. When our daughter was in kindergarten, her teacher told us that class parties at the school had gotten out of hand. Each kindergarten class had a room mother (the mom of one of the students) who was in charge of planning parties for events like Christmas, Valentine's Day, and the last day of school. All the teachers wanted were simple parties with cookies, soft drinks and a planned game or two. But as these mothers heard what other room moms were doing, they escalated things. Soon, they were bringing in catered food, elaborate activities and themed decorations. One class party even featured an ice sculpture. This was in a middle-class neighborhood, by the way.

If that story makes you shake your head (as I did), ask yourself, "What sorts of things do I consider necessities of life that would have been unheard-of when I was growing up?" In my childhood, we didn't have cable TV, even though it existed. Now, most of us feel that we must have multiple streaming packages. Of course, we take it for granted that every member of the family will have a smartphone, plus gaming devices (and the monthly costs for online access), subscriptions to premium music services, and the list goes on. And that's just our media. What about the sorts of clothes we buy? Or the restaurants we frequent? Or the money we pay to Amazon Prime so that we can have our heart's desire within 24 hours? Or the kinds of cars we think we must have? And then there's the biggie: Our houses keep getting larger and more expensive. It's ironic that we're spending so much to provide our families with what we think will produce happiness. In reality, as each family member withdraws to our own spaces in our huge houses, earbuds inserted as we enjoy our own personal entertainment, what we're really buying is the ability to get away from each other. What we call "providing" can literally isolate us from the people we are supposed to love.

Greed is an accepted part of our culture. There is an old saying: "The last thing in the world a fish will notice is water." One reason we're unlikely to see our own money-worship is that our world is so saturated in it. We can't imagine what it would be like to live without that constant craving for more. Just look at the daily barrage of advertising we face. Companies have a very specific strategy, as theologian Michael Horton observes:

"One marketing professor explains, 'There are only two ways to increase customers. Either you switch them to your brand or you grow them from birth.' The president of a chain of children's specialty stores says, 'All of these people understand something that is very basic and logical, that if you own this child at an early age, you can own this child for years to come. Companies are saying, Hey, I want to own the kid younger and younger and younger.' A General Mills executive adds, 'When it comes to targeting kid consumers, we at General Mills follow the Proctor & Gamble model of 'cradle to grave.' We believe in getting them early and having them for life.' Finally, the president of a leading ad agency declares, 'Advertising at its best is making people feel that without their produce, you're a loser. Kids are very sensitive to that. … You open up emotional vulnerabilities, and it's very easy to do with kids because they're the most emotionally vulnerable."

We may not be kids, but we're just as vulnerable to this messaging. Our culture is telling us not to settle for what we have, to reject contentment in favor of greed.

Greed is baked-in to our sin nature. We are ridiculous creatures. We see a new luxury sedan in our neighbor's driveway, and suddenly begin to hate our own car. Sure, it's reliable (and even better, almost paid off!), but don't we deserve better than that old piece of junk? We show up to a dinner party looking our best, but when we see a friend wearing something brand new and expensive, we feel unattractive. Immediately, a once-enjoyable night becomes a depressing experience. We hear that our co-worker took a vacation to Cancun. Our family vacation, on the other hand, was to a water park on the other side of the state. We had a great time, but now we wonder, "Why can't I go to a tropical paradise?" Logically, none of this makes sense. Shouldn't we be thrilled to have a car of our own, a closet full of clothes, and the ability to travel for fun? Most people on earth today have none of those things, and would consider anyone who did spectacularly wealthy. We're unhappy because of our sin nature, which won't let us enjoy the blessings God has given us. This is why the Ninth Commandment reads, *You shall not covet your neighbor's house; you shall not covet your neighbor's wife, or his male servant, or his female servant, or his ox, or his donkey, or anything that is your neighbor's* (Exodus 20:17). God knew we would be prone to play the toxic game of comparison, and He wanted to spare us that pain. Yet it seems to come so naturally to us, we think our coveting is legitimate, instead of sinful.

Jesus and Money

I've heard preachers say, "Jesus talked more about money than he did about Heaven and Hell combined." I haven't done the math to see if that is true. But I do know two things: First, Jesus spoke more often about money and possessions than you might expect from a man who was essentially unemployed and homeless. And second, He wasn't telling His crowds—or us—how to get rich. Here's a good example of Jesus' style of money teaching, found in Luke 12:13-21:

13 Someone in the crowd said to him, "Teacher, tell my brother to divide the inheritance with me." 14 But he said to him, "Man, who made me a judge or arbitrator over you?" 15 And he said to them, "Take care, and be on your guard against all covetousness, for one's life does not consist in the abundance of his possessions." 16 And he told them a parable, saying, "The land of a rich man produced plentifully, 17 and he thought to himself, 'What shall I do, for I have nowhere to store my crops?' 18 And he said, 'I will do this: I will tear down my barns and build larger ones, and there I will store all my grain and my goods. 19 And I will say to my soul, "Soul, you have ample goods laid up for many years; relax, eat, drink, be merry."' 20 But God said to him, 'Fool! This night your soul is required of you, and the things you have prepared, whose will they be?' 21 So is the one who lays up treasure for himself and is not rich toward God."

Jesus calls this man a fool for doing something which our culture endorses…working hard and saving up his money to make a secure, comfortable life for himself. So let's get the obvious question out of the way first. Is it wrong to work hard and invest well? In a word: No. Scripture often criticizes the lazy person and the one who fails to plan ahead, and it's apparent God chooses to make some of His people wealthy by earthly standards (Abraham and Solomon are two examples). The rich fool's sin wasn't in getting rich. His sin wasn't even in building barns to store his grain--that's what the Bible calls good stewardship. His sin was in thinking that accumulating wealth was the purpose of life; that if he could make enough money to last the rest of his life, he would be happy. As usual, it's important to see the context in which Jesus told the parable. A young man has just approached Jesus asking for help in negotiating the terms of an inheritance with his brother. Jesus replies, "Who made me a judge between the two of you?" Essentially, Jesus is saying, "That's not my mission. I didn't come to help you get rich; I came to make you holy." Then He warned them, "Take care, and be on your guard against all covetousness, for one's life does not consist in the abundance of his possessions."

Jesus tells the story of the Rich Fool to prove His point: Giving in to our desire for more is spiritual suicide. Notice what God says in v. 21 (and by the way, this is the only parable Jesus ever told in which God Himself is a main character): So is the one who lays up treasure for himself and is not rich toward God. The rich man thought that if He made enough money, he would be set for the future. He didn't realize that money and possessions don't do a bit of good for the future. It's not OUR money and stuff, after all. It's just on loan to us. This is a tough lesson for us to get through our heads as Americans. To us, success means having more stuff than our parents had, or more stuff than our neighbors have. "Downsizing" is an ugly word; it means failure. Jesus in this parable is saying, "If you're rich in things of this world and not rich toward God, you'll lose your soul."

Losing Our Souls

What does the worship of money do to us?

Makes us miserable. John D Rockefeller was the richest man in the world. How rich? At the peak of his wealth, Rockefeller's net worth was approximately 1% of the US economy (he was the original "1 percenter!"). He owned over 90% of the oil and gas industry. One day, a reporter asked him, "Mr. Rockefeller, how much money is enough?" "A little more," he answered. That may be the only thing you and I have in common with a billionaire. No matter how much we get, greed makes us think it's not enough; that real happiness is within reach, if only we can add just a little more to our bottom line. In the Greek myth of Sisyphus, a mortal is condemned by the gods to push a bolder up a hill. But every time he reaches the top of the hill, the bolder rolls back to the bottom. When we worship money, that's the way we live. The average American is living under the burden of over $5000 in credit card debt (in Texas, it's worse—over $6000). As a nation, our total consumer debt (including mortgages, car notes, student loans and credit card debt) is over $14.9 trillion. Instead of paying down that debt, we add to it every time we see something we can't live without. So we work harder and harder, and that bolder keeps rolling back down the hill.

Damages families. Just outside the majestic walls of Jerusalem's Old City, there's a valley called Ben Hinnom. In Aramaic, it was called Gehenna. That's the name Jesus used as a metaphor for Hell. The first time I ever visited Israel, our guide took us there. There is nothing to see; just a gently sloping valley with a few wildflowers (we were there in March). Yet he reminded us that during Old Testament times, that valley was the place where the people of Judah engaged in child sacrifice. Imagine men and women who knew the God of love and light, offering their own children in fires dedicated to pagan deities like Molech. In spite of the peacefulness of the place, I felt eerie chills knowing what had happened there. When we read these stories in Scripture, we wonder how parents could even consider doing such awful things. But how many parents today sacrifice their children's lives on the altar of wealth? How many moms and dads abdicate their responsibility to be the prime spiritual influencers in the lives of their kids in their most formative years, because they're too busy chasing an upscale lifestyle? How many marriages are torn apart because of disputes about money?

Warps our theology. If you look at the most popular Christian books or podcasts, you will find that many are produced by preachers of the "Prosperity Gospel." Obviously, that's not a term any of these Christian celebrities claim for themselves. But it's an apt term nonetheless. They take verses of Scripture out of context to convince us that God's raison d'etre is to give us what we want; that the goal of the Christian life is to become wealthier and healthier than our neighbors. It turns the Almighty, Sovereign God into nothing more than a cosmic butler. Instead of weaning us off of toxic traits like self-centeredness and envy, it enshrines them as virtues. And it ignores the many things the Bible says about how God can use suffering and trials to grow us, and instead teaches us that if we suffer, it's our fault for not having enough faith. This warped theology could only thrive in an environment where wealth is our true god. Think about it: The person we are supposed to emulate is Jesus Christ, who wasn't trying to have His "Best Life Now," because He was too busy giving His life away.

The more we become like Jesus, the less we will think about our own earthly wealth and health, because we will be focused on loving others.

Hurts our communities. Imagine a preacher stood in the pulpit of the average Evangelical church and said the following: "Come now, you rich, weep and howl for the miseries that are coming upon you. Your riches have rotted and your garments are moth-eaten. Your gold and silver have corroded, and their corrosion will be evidence against you and will eat your flesh like fire. You have laid up treasure in the last days. Behold, the wages of the laborers who mowed your fields, which you kept back by fraud, are crying out against you, and the cries of the harvesters have reached the ears of the Lord of hosts." These words were written not by some Marxist revolutionary, but by the Lord's own brother in James 5:1-4. A greedy person doesn't just lose his own soul; he also poisons the lives of people whose names he doesn't even know.

Andrew Carnegie, the steel baron, recognized early in his career that he was susceptible to the dangers of greed. As he wrote in a memorandum to himself, "Man must have an idol—The amassing of wealth is one of the worst species of idolatry." He pledged to resign from business at the age of thirty-five (which was only two years away at the time). But the lure of more was too strong. Perhaps to assuage his guilt for breaking his vow to himself, Carnegie became one of the most famous philanthropists of all time. Our nation is covered with institutions and buildings (including 2059 libraries alone) that bear his name, over a century after his death. But one of his employees told an interviewer, "We didn't want him to build a library for us, we would rather have had higher wages." In his quest for greater profits, Carnegie worked his employees on twelve-hour shifts on floors so hot, they had to nail wood to the bottoms of their boots to keep their feet from burning. Wages were low, so workers had to live in crowded, unsanitary housing. Most died in their forties or earlier, either from workplace accidents, disease or other causes. Carnegie wasn't the last boss to hurt others in his quest for mammon. We still see companies as diverse as Walmart and Nike exposed for their unlivable wages or unjust working conditions.

Running a business, large or small, is complex on many levels.

It's easy for an author like me to urge business owners to be generous to their employees. After all, I don't have to answer to their shareholders or find ways to cover overhead without pricing my company out of business. In fact, you might say that my own greedy desire for more stuff at lower prices is what causes such cruelty. But it is a battle worth fighting. Dan Price was raised in a devout Christian home. During his college years, he started a company called Gravity Payments that soon made him a millionaire. One day, he realized that most of his employees couldn't afford to live in the city (Seattle) where his company was based. He then decided that every employee of Gravity Payments would make at least $70,000 a year. To make this feasible, he cut his own pay from $1.1 million to $70,000. In the five years after Price's decision, Gravity's business has tripled, and he now employs twice as many people. More importantly, Price says the lives of his employees have improved: They've eliminated debt, begun contributing to retirement accounts, bought homes, lost weight, and started families. Fifty babies were born to Gravity employees in the five years after the pay increases, compared to just 1-2 per year before.

Ends in heartbreak: Perhaps you've heard that "money is the root of all evil." That's not actually what the Bible says. But what it does say is far more convicting: *But those who desire to be rich fall into temptation, into a snare, into many senseless and harmful desires that plunge people into ruin and destruction. For the love of money is a root of all kinds of evils. It is through this craving that some have wandered away from the faith and pierced themselves with many pangs* (1 Timothy 2:9-10) . We simply must ask ourselves, "Do I believe God's word or not?" If the answer is yes, then we believe that the very desire to get rich is a trap that leads to destruction. We'll repent of a drive that our culture says is perfectly natural, even healthy. If we believe God's word, we'll do this knowing that we're really not sacrificing anything; life apart from the worship of mammon is where true joy is found. If the answer is no, then we'll wind up like the rich fool in Jesus' parable: Perhaps rich in the things of this world, but bankrupt in the things that matter.

The Simple Life is Better

My brother is an architect. About ten years ago, his firm began to get lots of jobs from local churches. What brought about this sudden ecclesiastical building boom? Oil companies, using the new technique of fracking, had found ways to get natural gas out of cow pastures that had long been considered dry. That meant that several small-time ranchers in that area were suddenly rich. As my brother put it, "None of these guys knew what to do with all that money. So most of them just bought themselves a new truck and gave the rest to their church." Now those churches were building gymnasiums, fellowship halls, food pantries, and other facilities to better serve their communities. The story made me laugh; Most people I know (including me) would have no problem at all finding ways to spend a six-figure check. Truth is, we'd run out of money long before we would run out of things to buy. But I grew up around people just like those ranchers. I think about my grandparents, who consistently tithed, gave generously to people and causes, and were constantly giving gifts and treating people to lunch. Grandpa was a dairy farmer, and Grandma was a housewife; how could they be so generous? They lived in a small house that had long been paid for. Their clothes and cars were chosen for utility, not for status. They didn't have any expensive hobbies. They were free to be generous. Every year when Christmas or birthdays approached, I would struggle to think of what to get Grandma and Grandpa; they didn't seem to want anything.

I'm not saying that everyone should live like my grandparents. But we can take steps to live simpler lives. In his classic, *Celebration of Discipline*, Richard Foster describes an ancient practice called the spiritual discipline of simplicity. This is voluntary downsizing, offloading some of the excess stuff that complicates our lives. I recommend reading the book for yourself, but here are some ways I've tried to put this discipline into practice:

Giving things away or throwing them away. If I have so much extra stuff that I have to pay to store it, I have too much stuff. If I have accumulated so much stuff that it's getting in the way of my relationships with other people, I need to get rid of it. If I am hanging on to stuff that would bless others, I need to give it away.

Pruning our budget of unnecessary bills. Do I really need cable TV AND Netflix? Do I really need to go on paying dues to a gym I never visit? Couldn't I be more generous if I lived with less?

Being honest with ourselves about our priorities. Do I dress the way I do to impress other people? Do I really need to own that new smartphone the day it comes out, or could I wait until it costs half as much? How much money do I waste on eating out because I don't take time to plan meals?

Examining our weekly commitments. Is there anything I could stop doing that would give me more time for serving God? Am I working so many extra hours because I have to, or because I want more stuff?

Foster says there are really two parts to the discipline of simplicity: It is an inward reality that results in an outward lifestyle. If we say we have the inward reality but don't have the outward lifestyle, we're deceiving ourselves. We're the guy who says, "Of course God is more important to me than wealth," but when someone or something threatens our stash, we lose our religion pretty quickly.

On the other hand, if we try to live the outward lifestyle of simplicity without changing on the inside, we become legalists. We're the guy who judges everyone else's possessions: "Anyone who drives a nicer car than me is a sinner. Anyone who eats out more often than me is selfish."

What is the inward reality we need? Jesus spoke to peasants who were worried about putting food on their tables, not about whether they should buy that pair of $200 jeans or upgrade their kitchen. Yet He had the audacity to say these words (Matthew 6:31-33):

31 Therefore do not be anxious, saying, 'What shall we eat?' or 'What shall we drink?' or 'What shall we wear?' 32 For the Gentiles seek after all these things, and your heavenly Father knows that you need them all. 33 But seek first the kingdom of God and his righteousness, and all these things will be added to you.

The inward reality we need is a constant mindset that says: "Jesus is my joy; Jesus is enough for me. If I need anything else in this world, He'll provide it." That's what it truly means to be "rich toward

God."

The Cure for Greed

How do we get that inward reality? In Luke 19, we read about a man who was so determined to be wealthy, he sold out his own people, becoming a tax collector for the enemy. It worked; Zacchaeus was eventually promoted to chief tax collector. But he was miserable in spite of his wealth. One day, he heard that Jesus was coming through his hometown of Jericho. He must have heard of this strange rabbi who was turning Israel on its ear, because Zacchaeus not only went out to see Jesus, he climbed into a tree to catch a glimpse of Him. This was humiliating for Zacchaeus, not only because it highlighted his short stature, but (how can I put this delicately?) because of the clothing men wore in those days, climbing a tree would expose a man's undercarriage to those walking below. We can be sure the citizens of Jericho, all of whom had been fleeced by Zacchaeus, were laughing their heads off at this stumpy crook hanging out of a sycamore, with his Fruit of the Looms showing. When Jesus saw the man, He stunned the crowd by saying, *Zacchaeus, hurry and come down, for I must stay at your house today*. Out of the thousands of hungry souls crowding the streets of Jericho that day, why would the Lord enter the home of the greediest person there? He must have recognized that this man was ready for a change. And so he was. Zacchaeus said, *Behold, Lord, the half of my goods I give to the poor. And if I have defrauded anyone of anything, I restore it fourfold.* Jesus responded by saying, *Today, salvation has come to this house.*

There are three things to note about this familiar story. First, Zacchaeus made an offer that was extraordinarily generous. The Law of Moses stipulated that any theft be repaid with an additional twenty percent added; for Zacchaeus to repay fourfold was well beyond what God required. Second, he didn't make this offer so that Jesus would accept him. In that culture, entering a person's home was a sign of full acceptance. Zacchaeus gave away his money out of thankfulness, not desperation. Third, think about the story of Jesus and the rich young ruler (Mark 10:17-22). Jesus told this young man that his wealth was the thing standing between him and true salvation. He said it, Mark tells us, not to make it hard for this young man to be saved, but because

Jesus loved him. The rich young ruler went away sad, because his wealth wouldn't share allegiance with anyone, even God incarnate. Zacchaeus, on the other hand, didn't have to be asked. Generosity welled up out of the joy in his heart. This man was truly saved.

The only thing that can cure our love of money is an encounter with the Son of God. And since the false god of mammon is so pervasive in our culture, we need to spend time in Christ's presence every single day, to remind ourselves of where our true wealth lies. After all, we live in a world that idolizes riches. Our favorite stories are of people who go from outhouse to penthouse. But we worship the ultimate rich guy who voluntarily became poor. *For you know the grace of our Lord Jesus Christ, that though he was rich, yet for your sake he became poor, so that you by his poverty might become rich* (2 Corinthians 8:9). He gave up what He had, taking on the worst of what we deserved, so we could inherit what belonged rightfully to Him. That is the model we follow. That is the Savior we serve. And He is more than enough.

Chapter 4

Planet Eros: The Idol of Sex and Romance

Imagine you live hundreds of years in the future, and you're studying 21st Century America, the way historians today study the Roman Empire or the Ming Dynasty. After watching hours of old movies and TV shows, examining page after page of social media posts, and dissecting the lyrics of our most popular songs, you come to a conclusion: "Americans in the 21st Century increasingly rejected organized religion, but they were still worshippers. Whereas many of their forefathers worshipped the God of the Bible, Americans in the 2000s worshipped romantic love and sex. They traded the ideal of a transforming relationship with a personal God for the dream of falling in love with their soul mate. They gave up hoping for eternal bliss in everlasting Heaven, in favor of seeking the transcendent experience of great sex."

You may think I'm overstating my case. But recently, I was waiting in my doctor's office, while a stream of country music played in the background. My ears perked up when I heard words that sounded like they belonged in a modern praise-and-worship anthem. With all the ambient noise in the office, it was hard to tell exactly what this catchy song was about, but I distinctly heard the three-fold repetition of the word "Holy, Holy, Holy" in the chorus. When I got home, I searched the song on the internet, and found the lyrics of a song called "H.O.L.Y." by Florida-Georgia Line. I was right: It most definitely is a worship song, but God is not the object of the singer's adoration. The title H.O.L.Y. stands for "High on loving you," as the chorus repeats several times. The verses are about the life-changing love our singer has found in a romantic relationship:

I sat in darkness, all broken hearted
I couldn't find a day I didn't feel alone
I never meant to cry, started losing hope
But somehow baby, you broke through and saved me

That sounds curiously like a Christian born-again testimony (aside from the fact that I've never heard a new believer refer to God as "baby"). And in fact, he goes on to call this spectacular woman, "the river bank where I was baptized." She has "cleansed all the demons that were killing my freedom." In return, he promises that his love will have her singing "Hallelujah," and that they'll be "touching heaven." He declares:

You're the healing hands where it used to hurt
You're my saving grace, you're my kind of church

Lest you think I'm picking on country music, I give you the song "Take me to Church," by Irish alternative rocker Hozier:

I should've worshiped her sooner
If the Heavens ever did speak
She's the last true mouthpiece

My church offers no absolutes
She tells me, "Worship in the bedroom"
The only Heaven I'll be sent to
Is when I'm alone with you
I was born sick, but I love it
Command me to be well
Amen, Amen, Amen

Take me to church
I'll worship like a dog at the shrine of your lies
I'll tell you my sins and you can sharpen your knife
Offer me that deathless death

Good God, let me give you my life

The ancient Greek word for romantic desire was *eros*, from which we get our English word "erotic." The Greeks even had a god named Eros, who was their version of Cupid. Most of us today have grown up being thoroughly discipled by our culture in the ways of Eros, leaving us with two basic doctrines we hold with religious fervor:

Eros doctrine number one: Sex is an inalienable right. We've been taught that sex is the ultimate human experience. Our worst fear is to die a virgin, or be doomed to a sexually boring marriage, never having summited the Mount Everest of earthly pleasures. Therefore, anyone who criticizes or condemns our consensual sexual relationships is our enemy. Any rule or creed that denies us the right to sleep with whomever we choose is outdated, or even deliberately repressive.

Eros doctrine number two: My soulmate exists. Somewhere on earth right now is a person who can fulfill your physical and emotional needs in a way that will make your fondest dreams come true. All the old stories tell us so: Cinderella has her Prince Charming. Aragorn has his Arwen. Rose has her Jack (okay, bad example). Sure, plenty of people reject that kind of aching romanticism, but most still feel, deep in their hearts, that if they could fall in love with the right kind of person, that relationship would be enough to overcome the tragedies and disappointments of life.

The Marital Prosperity Gospel

Like the ancient Israelites, who often combined the worship of Yahweh with visits to the shrine of the local fertility god, modern American Christianity developed its own version of Eros worship. I got married three decades ago, at the start of a new marriage movement in Christianity. The sexual revolution of the 1960s had torn down many of the traditional expectations about marriage and sex. By the 1990s, when I was getting married, evangelical authors and speakers were fighting back. Whereas before, churches were prudish places when it came to discussions of the erotic sort, now they began to sell a consistent message: If you marry a Christian, and you save yourself physically for marriage, you're guaranteed marital bliss for life…including torridly satisfying sex.

In Joel Gregory's book about his tenure at First Baptist, Dallas, *Too Great a Temptation*, he mentions a sermon his predecessor, WA Criswell once preached. Dr. Criswell was pastor at FBC for fifty years. With his white mane of hair, his tailored suit and his commanding voice, he looked like the kind of man who could truly speak for God. On this particular day, he wanted to urge young people to do things God's way. So he referenced some recent studies about marital satisfaction among Christians, baptized them in Scripture, and his money line was, "Young men, marry a First Baptist woman. She'll love you so good, they'll have to carry you off in a wheelbarrow." The huge congregation was stunned into silence at this unexpectedly saucy declaration. But then they blew the roof off with laughter. That was forevermore known as "the wheelbarrow sermon." Interestingly, Gregory reports that when people asked Mrs. Criswell what she thought of it, she said, "WA doesn't know what he's talking about."

By the early 2000s, such a sermon wouldn't have been unusual at all. Sermons on the allurements of Christian marriage were commonplace in evangelical churches. Congregations could expect their pastor to take the lead, with occasional references to his "Smokin' hot wife" giving the unmistakable cue that the Marital Prosperity Gospel worked. Ed Young Jr. famously preached a series about sex and marriage while sitting on a bed placed provocatively on the church stage. Mark Driscoll often told the women of his Seattle megachurch that their job was to get married, have kids, and satisfy their husbands sexually. Many others followed in their footsteps.

All You Need Is Love?

One result of all of this is that Christians are just as likely to worship Eros as unbelievers. Here are some of the ways this has impacted our culture, both inside and outside the Church:

Kids and teenagers in America grow up in a hyper-sexualized pop-culture world. Most have access to entertainment and social media that presents an unquestioned assumption about sex: Everyone's doing it. By the time an American kid turns 18, two-thirds of her peers have had sexual intercourse.[i] While she may feel like the odd one out, most of her sexually-experienced peers (67% overall, and 77% of girls) say they wish they had waited longer.[ii] Premarital sex— and its many potential consequences—aren't the only problem, either. Chances are, all of us can name teenagers who've been in possessive, obsessive, emotionally-scarring dating relationships. In fact, I'll bet many of us can tell such stories about our own teenaged selves. The myth of Eros—the idea that meeting your true love will change your life forever for good—seems especially appealing to our minds at this age, and it can lead us into a world of pain.

Women today are much more liberated than their ancestors, and for that, we should all be thankful. Even so, how many women continue to measure themselves by their perceived attractiveness to men? Many otherwise intelligent, capable women stay in terrible, even abusive relationships because they can't face the idea of being alone. Others compromise their own moral standards to win the affections of a man who they hope will make them feel worthwhile. That's to say nothing of eating disorders and the other self-harming things that women by the millions do to their bodies in pursuit of some elusive standard of beauty. And it's to say nothing of the 42 million women worldwide who are in prostitution today[iii], or the over 4 million women and girls estimated to be victims of sex trafficking globally.

Of course, most women manage to avoid these terrible fates. But that doesn't mean our culture's fixation on romantic love leaves them unscathed. Here's just one example: In my time in the ministry, I've seen weddings grow more and more expensive. According to The Knot website, the average cost of a wedding in 2020 was $19,000—and that's down from previous years, since COVID-19 caused weddings to be scaled back. When I do premarital counseling, I try to convince couples to consider a smaller wedding. "You'll be just as married!" I tell them. But many brides feel an enormous pressure to live up to the lavish expectations of their family and friends (and, let's be honest, their own fairy-tale dreams since girlhood). It's a tough way to enter the most important human relationship of one's life—sunk in wedding debt combined with unrealistic hopes of "happily ever after."

Men are just as likely to idolize Eros. Whenever a man asks to speak to me privately, regardless of his age, marital status, or any other factor, I expect the subject of porn use to come up. That's how common it is. I've seen studies that claim 80% of men look at porn weekly[iv], and I don't doubt them. While scientists disagree on whether pornography is addictive, I can only tell you the destructive effects it has on marriages, mental health, and the ability of men to have healthy relationships. It's not just images on a screen, either. A few years ago, the #MeToo movement burst onto our national consciousness, dethroning famous, powerful men in such rapid succession it was hard to keep up. Movie stars, politicians, athletes, preachers…no man was safe, not even Bill Cosby. For me, Cosby was the most disheartening case. I grew up watching *Fat Albert* cartoons and laughing at Cosby's standup routines (including his series about Noah and the Ark) on cassette. *The Cosby Show* was must-see TV at my house on Thursday nights as a teenager. But at the same time this man was building a reputation as "America's Dad," and lecturing comedians like Richard Pryor and Eddie Murphy for using profanity, he was drugging and raping women by the dozens (so far, 60 have accused him). MeToo has faded, but the problem remains; 1 in 6 women will experience some form of sexual assault in their lifetime[v]. Many others will be stalked, shamed, abused or harassed by men as diverse as bosses and would-be boyfriends. No social media campaign can change this.

Eros worship fills a man with a sense of entitlement: the idea that women exist for his own enjoyment.

Single adults, both male and female, face intense social pressure to "settle down and get married." This is especially true in the church. Whenever I mention Paul's teachings about Christian singleness from 1 Corinthians 7 in a sermon (see below), I always have at least one single person over 30 who thanks me profusely. They're so tired of hearing, "Have you found someone yet?" In college, I was part of a Christian organization which had a single woman on its staff. She told me about the Mother's Day when her pastor said in his sermon, "If you're a woman, being a mother is the greatest thing you can ever do with your life." Since she had no plans to be married or have kids, it seemed clear that her church thought she was living a second-class life, no matter how dedicated she was to serving Christ. Outside the church, of course, people like her would be even less accepted, since their commitment to lifelong celibacy would seem absurd.

Getting married isn't the answer, either. No man or woman can possibly fulfill us in the way Eros promises. As a result, many married people find themselves deeply disillusioned. Some even wonder if their true soulmate is out there, somewhere else. As I mentioned earlier, I got married in the early 1990s, just as the Marital Prosperity Gospel was taking root in evangelical life. Based on all I had been told, I believed I was destined for marital bliss. I had found a good Christian girl, and we'd saved ourselves sexually for marriage. We got married the week after we graduated college; I didn't want to wait a day longer than I had to. The night before the wedding, I was so excited, I literally didn't sleep at all. Soon after the wedding, I realized this was going to be harder than I thought. We were fighting...a lot. I was stunned. I couldn't figure out where we'd gone wrong. Today, 30 years later, I actually thank God for those early days of struggle. They showed me that my wife, wonderful as she is, can never bear the weight of my worship. That realization, that process of weaning me from Eros-worship, has made all the difference.

There's a lovestruck young man in the Bible who reminds me of myself. His name is Jacob; He's the son of Isaac, grandson of Abraham and Sarah, and in Genesis 29, he meets the woman of his dreams.

Now Laban had two daughters. The name of the older was Leah, and the name of the younger was Rachel. Leah's eyes were weak, but Rachel was beautiful in form and appearance. Jacob loved Rachel. And he said, "I will serve you seven years for your younger daughter Rachel." Laban said, "It is better that I give her to you than that I should give her to any other man; stay with me." So Jacob served seven years for Rachel, and they seemed to him but a few days because of the love he had for her (Genesis 29:16-20).

In that time, fathers controlled the marriages of their children. For a man with a daughter as attractive as Rachel, that could lead to some financial opportunities. Jacob decided to bid high: He offered to work for Laban for seven years with no other prize than the hand of his daughter. Let's put that into perspective: Since the median US salary today is $60,000, Jacob is offering Laban $420,000 for his daughter. Verse 20 says those seven years *seemed to him but a few days because of the love he had for her*. That's as romantic as anything you'll ever read. That's Jacob saying, "You complete me," and Rachel saying, "You had me at hello." Tim Keller's excellent book *Counterfeit Gods* has a whole chapter on this story. He points out that when Jacob says to Laban in verse 21, *"Give me my wife that I may go in to her, for my time is completed,"* it's an incredibly graphic thing for someone to say out loud. He's essentially saying, "I can't wait to sleep with your daughter!" Who says that? Only someone who's so in love, he has lost all common sense.

Scripture and Eros

What does the Bible say? It says that God created marriage, and He created sex. For instance, do you know what the first command in Scripture is? Genesis 1:28, *Be fruitful and multiply*. What did Adam and Eve have to do in order to obey that command? Yes, that's right: God's first command was telling a husband and wife to have sex. We think of marriage today as a legal institution, involving both the church and the state. But when God made marriage, it was as simple as a man and a woman becoming *one flesh* (Genesis 2:24).

Years ago, a man said to me, "Christianity teaches that sex is for reproduction only, not for pleasure. So you can only have sex when you're actively trying to have kids." I replied, "I have read the Bible several times, and I am not aware of that teaching anywhere in it. And if you know where it is, please don't tell my wife!" I have no idea where he got this idea, but the notion that Christianity is sexually repressive doesn't square with what the Bible actually says. In frank, often earthy terms, God's Word urges us to enjoy our physical relationship with our spouse. Proverbs 5:18-19, for instance, advises husbands: *May your fountain be blessed, and may you rejoice in the wife of your youth. A loving doe, a graceful deer, may her breasts satisfy you always; may you ever be captivated by her love.* There is not room here to quote the entire Song of Solomon, but let me sum it up for you: This is an entire book of the Bible dedicated to describing the erotic relationship between a husband and wife. So when married people take pleasure in each other's bodies, they are actually obeying God. When we seek the sexual fulfillment of our spouse, it pleases the One who made us.

In fact, God's attitude toward marital sex is "practice makes perfect." 1 Corinthians 7:3-4 reads, *The husband should fulfill his marital duty to his wife, and likewise the wife to her husband. The wife's body does not belong to her alone but also to her husband. In the same way, the husband's body does not belong to him alone but also to his wife. Do not deprive one another except by mutual consent and for a time, so that you may devote yourself to prayer.* Just to be clear: That command should be read in the context of love. Love does not force itself on anyone, and no man should ever coerce his wife (physically or emotionally) to do what she doesn't want to do. What it does show is that mutually fulfilling sex is part of a healthy love relationship.

As beautiful and enjoyable as this gift is, however, it can also be dangerous. 1 Corinthians 6:18-20 warns: *Flee from sexual immorality. All other sins a person commits are outside the body, but whoever sins sexually, sins against their own body. Do you not know that your bodies are temples of the Holy Spirit, who is in you, whom you have received from God? You are not your own; you were bought at a price. Therefore honor God with your bodies.* Paul doesn't define "sexual immorality" here, because he didn't need to. All of his first-century readers knew that the clear, unequivocal teaching of Scripture was that sex was created by God for one relationship only: The marriage of a man and a woman. This flies in the face of our culture's current thinking, in which any relationship between consenting adults must be not only accepted, but celebrated. Some see Biblical teaching as being "On the wrong side of history." But if Jesus is the King of the Universe, His side is always, ultimately the right side of history.

Paul wasn't saying that sinning sexually changes how God feels about us. But he was saying it affects us differently than other sins. Sex is more than the fulfilling of a physical desire, like eating or sleeping. Something happens in the act of sex that doesn't happen anywhere else. Deep down, we all know this to be true. Why else are the criminal penalties for rape different from those for simple assault? Because we all acknowledge that a person who has been violated sexually faces a different type of trauma than someone who has bruises or a broken bone. The body heals, but when we rob someone of the right to share that intimate act willingly, lovingly, we have wounded their soul. If that is true when sex is forcibly taken, it is also true when it is casually given away. God made our bodies for certain purposes. When we use our bodies in ways they were never designed to be used, there are consequences.

Yet it's also interesting to note how many times Jesus encountered people who were seen as "dirty" because they had fallen short of God's standards when it came to sexuality. In every case—whether He was stopping an accused adulteress from being stoned to death by an angry mob, forgiving a "sinful woman" who had tearfully anointed Him with costly oil, or responding to charges that He was a friend of prostitutes—Jesus gave them dignity. He showed them grace. He restored them instead of consigning them to life's dustbin. Over the last two thousand years, the followers of Jesus have often treated sexual sins as unforgivable, but Jesus never did…and never will.

Jesus famously said in Matthew 5:27-28, *You have heard that it was said, 'You shall not commit adultery.' But I tell you that anyone who looks at a woman lustfully has already committed adultery with her in his heart.* I need to point out three things about that command: First, the responsibility is on men to govern how they look at women, not on women to avoid tempting men. There is a place for a discussion of modesty, but that's not what Jesus is talking about here. Religious movements that put the onus of responsibility on women, who treat women as if their bodies are shameful, who legislate what clothes women are allowed to wear, are not operating in the Spirit of Christ. Jesus didn't tell women to wrap themselves in burlap from nose to toes; He told men to take responsibility for their eyes and thoughts. Second, this command shows how seriously God takes our sexual thoughts, as well as our actions. Third, think of the terrible evils that could be avoided if men obeyed this one command. Imagine a world in which every man looked at every woman through eyes of respect and love, as a fellow image-bearer of God, not as a source of gratification or a potential conquest. That's a world without Eros worship.

Although God created marriage, He doesn't hold it up as the highest possible good, or even something that is designed for every person. Jesus was a lifelong celibate man, and He lived the fullest, most meaningful life in human history. The Apostle Paul, also, was unmarried. In 1 Corinthians 7, he wrote to tell young Christians that marriage was a good thing. But in verses 6 and 7, he adds this interesting caveat: *I say this as a concession, not as a command. I wish that all of you were as I am. But each of you has your own gift from God; one has this gift, another has that.* Far from wondering when he would meet his soulmate, Paul considered his singleness a gift. He thought he was better able to serve God fully—and therefore live out the divine purpose for which he was created—without having to worry about taking care of a wife and children. In my life, I have been blessed to be friends with many amazing Christian men and women who lived their entire lives unmarried. Some in this group are people who feel attracted to others of their same gender. They believe that a celibate life in obedience to God brings them more joy and fulfillment than allowing their desires to rule. By refusing to be defined by their sexuality, they stand faithfully and courageously against the cult of Eros that rules so many of us.

This all culminates in the transcendent words of Ephesians 5. After telling husbands in v. 25 to *love your wives as Christ loved the church, laying down His life for her,* then explaining that our job as husbands is to sanctify our wives, to help them live out their full God-given potential (a revolutionary teaching in a world in which wives were seen as the virtual property of their husbands). He then says in v. 32, *This mystery is profound, and I am saying that it refers to Christ and the church.* Paul, a celibate man who treasured his singleness, was saying that God chose marriage to be the picture of His love for us. When a married couple loves each other the way God intended, it shows the world our future. Jesus constantly compared His Second Coming to a wedding feast. The story of humanity, which began with a couple losing their home, ends with a wedding…and a loving marriage that never ends.

Jacob, Rachel…and the other sister

Romantic love and sex are celebrated in Scripture as blessings from God, but they cannot be the goal of life. No person can be your salvation. Jacob found this out the hard way…and so did another person in his story. Jacob came from a very dysfunctional family. His father preferred Jacob's twin brother, Esau, to him. Jacob and his mother, Rebekah, schemed to steal the family blessing from Esau. When Esau found out, he swore to kill Jacob, who then ran away from home. So Jacob had been rejected, but then he found in Rachel the love he'd always been looking for. Laban had other ideas. He had an unattractive older daughter named Leah, and he was worried he'd never be able to find a husband for her. In that case, he would have to take care of Leah for the rest of his life. So on the wedding night, when Jacob was drunk, he sent Leah, heavily veiled, into Jacob's tent. When Jacob woke up the next morning, hung over, and saw the wrong woman in his bed, he confronted his father in law. Then Laban sprung the trap. "Oh, I assumed you knew that the oldest always gets married first. But if you still want Rachel, you can have her next week...but you'll work seven more years for me." So now the total cost to Jacob is $840,000. Jacob says yes.

Genesis 29:30 says, *So Jacob went in to Rachel also, and he loved Rachel more than Leah, and served Laban for another seven years.* Notice that it doesn't say that these seven years were like a few days. Actually being married to Rachel wasn't nearly as exciting as the anticipation of their marriage had been. The forgotten one in this story is Leah. Back in v. 16, it describes her as having "weak eyes." Since it's contrasted with Rachel's beauty, this isn't a reference to Leah's eyesight. Maybe it means she was cross-eyed, or it's an obscure way to say she "wasn't easy on the eyes." Either way, she lived her whole life in the shadow of her gorgeous little sister. Now she was sharing a husband with that sister, and that husband didn't love her. Keller calls her "the girl no one wanted." But Leah had a plan. In that culture, a woman had very few opportunities to use her intelligence or talents to advance herself. But if she could have children, especially sons, that might win her husband's love...especially when it turned out that Rachel seemed to be barren. So Leah had three babies in rapid succession, while Rachel remained childless. Did it work? Verses 31-34 tell us:

And Leah conceived and bore a son, and she called his name Reuben, for she said, "Because the LORD has looked upon my affliction; for now my husband will love me." She conceived again and bore a son, and said, "Because the LORD has heard that I am hated, he has given me this son also." And she called his name Simeon. Again she conceived and bore a son, and said, "Now this time my husband will be attached to me, because I have borne him three sons." Therefore his name was called Levi.

Leah gave Jacob what every man in his culture valued the most: Sons. The names she gave those sons betrayed her intention to win her husband's affection. It didn't work. This is the lie of Eros: "If I can only make this person love me, then I will be somebody." It's the same lie believed by the teenaged boy who attempts suicide after a breakup; the teenaged girl whose boyfriend says, "If you really love me, you'll do it;" the abused wife who stays because "he's really sweet sometimes;" the husband who finds his soulmate in another woman, only to end up with a shattered family and a shame he can't shake, realizing too late that all those books and movies about the glories of forbidden love are fool's gold.

The exit ramp from Eros-worship

Leah finally gave up on trying to win her man. Genesis 29:35 says, *And she conceived again and bore a son, and said, "This time I will praise the LORD." Therefore she called his name Judah.*
With her fourth baby, she didn't say, "I hope this makes my husband love me!" Instead, she said, "This time, I will praise the Lord." She said, "I'm never going to find the happiness I'm looking for in my marriage. So I will focus on praising God instead." The baby she had was named Judah. Many years later, when Jacob was an old man and he was blessing his twelve sons, who would be the patriarchs of the new people group known as the Jews, he singled out one of his sons as the one whose line would produce great kings, and even a Messiah. It wasn't Reuben, his firstborn. It wasn't even Joseph or Benjamin, the sons that Rachel finally conceived. No, it was Judah, the lion's cub, the son of Leah. Later, God brought forth His Messiah, Jesus, from

the tribe of Judah. Even if Jacob never loved Leah, God did. God is the lover of the unloved.

Just like Jacob, on my wedding day, I was convinced I was on the verge of unfiltered bliss. But I have this in common with Leah: One day, I realized that I had turned romantic love into something it was never meant to be. I was looking to my wife to do for me what only God could do. If I kept it up, I would destroy our marriage and myself. I had been a Christian most of my life; I thought I was a pretty good guy. But at that point, for the first time, I started seeking God not so that He would give me what I wanted, but simply because I had nothing else. I began studying His Word and praying like a man clinging to a life saver in the middle of the sea. And I grew like never before. I learned how to know what God was saying to me, and how to have a real relationship with Him. I prayed over and over again for Him to help me stop trying to change my wife, and instead to make me the kind of person I needed to be to make our marriage work.

So if you're single, let me say this: Sex is a gift from God, and marriage is a beautiful thing, but you don't need either one to live a fulfilling life. Instead of focusing on finding your soul mate (who doesn't exist) focus on becoming the person God made you to be, and take advantage of the opportunities to serve Him in ways that a married person like me cannot. If you do decide to get married, don't marry because you found someone physically attractive; don't marry because you are afraid of being alone. Marry because you find someone who makes you a better person, someone who inspires you to seek after God more fervently, who is strong in some of the ways you are weak, and who you can serve God alongside for a lifetime. If you're dating someone and wonder if he or she is that kind of person, ask people who will tell you the truth, and listen to them. But right now, lay your life before God and say, "Whether I marry or not, let me always find my true joy, identity and purpose in you."

If you are married, let me say this: There is one person God has for you, and it's the person you are currently married to. Do you know that in societies where marriages are arranged by parents, people report more marital satisfaction than in cultures like ours, where people marry for romantic love? The reason is obvious: A man in an arranged marriage knows that he is stuck with this woman, so he might as well learn to love her for who she is. He has no reason to compare her to some mythical person who meets all his needs; he went into the relationship without those overly romantic expectations. So whereas the American model leaves him thinking, "I must have married the wrong person," his actual situation leaves him with one viable option: Love the one he has. Build something beautiful with her. So lay your life before God. Ask Him to change you into the person you need to be in order for your marriage to work. And start seeking Him with your whole heart, knowing only He can give you what you truly need.

Why would you trust Him instead of the promises of romantic love and sex? Because no one else ever did for you what He did. He was the King of the Universe, adored by angels. He gave all that up to become the man no one wanted. He was physically unattractive and rejected by His own people (Isaiah 52 and 53). He laid down His life to save yours. If the most powerful being in the Universe would do that for you, is there anything He wouldn't do? You can trust Him.

Chapter 5

Snake Oil Savior: The Idol of Comfort

Up until about a hundred years ago, there was big money made in our country through what were known as "patent medicines." They were also known as "snake oil," because they often claimed to be made from exotic-sounding ingredients that supposedly cured any ailment. So one day, a medicine show would arrive in your town: A wagon would stop in the town square, and a little show would commence, with music, jugglers, magic tricks or feats of strength. In a time before our contemporary digital entertainment, such a show would bring people by the hundreds from miles around. Then the snake oil salesman would step forward and tell you about his wonderful elixir that could cure heartburn, headaches, coughing, cataracts, "female complaints," you name it. More successful patent medicines would advertise in national magazines. Then the federal government started regulating medicines, and most of the patent medicine folks went out of business. Others stopped marketing themselves as medicines, and some still exist today, like Coca Cola, Dr Pepper, and 7-Up. Think about that the next time you enjoy a soft drink: People once paid top dollar for a bottle of a product like this, thinking it would solve what was wrong with their bodies or brains, and that it would make their lives wonderful.

There are still snake-oil salesmen, and we're still buying products that don't work. You may remember a few years ago when "toning shoes" were very popular. These looked like regular athletic shoes, except the sole of the shoe was rounded instead of flat. Supposedly, this feature forced you to use muscles you wouldn't ordinarily use, so that you would lose weight and sculpt shapelier legs without actually working out. But clinical tests showed that toning shoes were useless. Many of us spent outlandish sums of money, only to end up just as flabby as before while wearing a pair of dorky-looking sneakers. A much bigger disaster happened a few years earlier, when Frito Lay produced WOW! Chips, made with Olestra, a compound that made chips taste just as good, but with no fat and very few calories. It was every snack-food junkie's dream come true! Unfortunately, Olestra turned out to be like a terrorist attack on many people's gastrointestinal system. So yes, you could eat Cool Ranch Doritos by the bagful and lose weight at the same time, but only because you were running to the bathroom every half hour.

But the ultimate snake-oil salesman is the god of comfort. Like most other idols, comfort can be a very good thing. It is a gift from God; in 2 Corinthians 1:3 He is called *the God of all comfort*. At the beginning of creation, God created the Sabbath day as a way of reminding us that we need to rest from our labors, so that we don't burn out (Exodus 20:8-10). When Jesus raised a little girl from the dead, the first thing He told her parents was, "Give this child something to eat" (Mark 5:43). I find it fascinating that He was the first to realize that this child, who had been in a coma for quite some time, would feel hungry. He cared about her comfort. Jesus also promised us that when we were weary and burdened down, we could come to Him and we would find rest for our souls (Matthew 11:28-30). He wants to take away our anxiety. He wants to comfort us, not simply save our souls. James tells us every good and perfect gift comes from above, from the Father of lights (James 1:17), so that means that anything enjoyable in life is a gift from God. That means we can worship God not simply through singing songs or listening to sermons; it's actually an act of worship to enjoy good food, good company, good music or other good things with thankfulness in our hearts toward God. He loves to see His children enjoy His gifts, like any other good Father. No wonder He is the God of all comfort!

Comfort becomes an idol when we make those good things into ultimate things. The idol of comfort says, "There is a way to eliminate all pain, stress and discomfort from life. You deserve that. You shouldn't settle for less." But God knows that's snake oil. He tells us so, over and over again in His word. John 16:33 says *In the world you will have tribulation. But take heart; I have overcome the world.* Philippians 1:29 says, *For it has been granted to you that for the sake of Christ you should not only believe in him but also suffer for his sake.* Not only does the Bible guarantee that there will be some pain in our lives, it says that it is "for Christ's sake." Scripture makes it clear that God doesn't necessarily cause all pain to happen, but He can use it to draw us closer to Him. Both Peter and Paul wrote about "sharing in the fellowship of Christ's suffering," meaning that when we experience pain, we are experiencing a small taste of what Jesus went through for us on the cross, and that helps us know Him better.

There's even a religious component: The idol of comfort whispers, "If God loves you, He'll protect you from pain. He'll give you the comfortable life you want, the life you deserve." So when pain enters our lives, we feel betrayed by God. I visited with a man once who told me that if I ever talked about how God uses suffering to grow us, he would quit coming to my church. He said, "If I had kids, I wouldn't want them to suffer. I would want only good things for them. I expect God to be the same way toward me." The problem with his analogy is that as a parent, I don't try to keep my children from all suffering. I don't enjoy watching them struggle, but I also don't swoop in to rescue them whenever life gets hard. I want to provide for them; I want them to be happy and comfortable, but my main job is to equip them to live for God in the world. I know that some hardships will actually help prepare them for life. God does the same for us. Tragically, that man later took his own life. I am convinced he was a victim of the snake oil that the false god of comfort offers.

The Snake-Oil Catalogue

It's important for us to recognize some of the signs of comfort idolatry in the world around us…and in ourselves.

Hedonism: Here's a good definition of hedonism: "The ethical theory that pleasure is the highest good and the proper aim of human life." I doubt any of us would admit that pleasure-seeking is the guiding philosophy of our lives. But think about how often our desire for pleasure steers us into decisions and behaviors that are the opposite of what Christ wants for us:

- Two-thirds of adults in our country are overweight, but we make almost all of our food choices based on what tastes good, not what is good for our bodies. Our supersized desires are causing us to literally eat ourselves to death.

- Our commitment to our hobbies and interests is cult-like. We spend massive amounts of money on sports and entertainment. Here's just one stunning fact: In two-thirds of US states, the highest-paid public employee is a college football coach. I'm a football fan myself, but that is a sure sign of a society with its priorities out of whack. But we don't need statistics to show us how our hobbies control our lives. If you're a golfer, think about how you feel if something happens (weather, getting called into work, the tearful request of a spouse) to cancel your game. If you're a video gamer, consider your mood when your internet is down. If you love your pets, imagine your state of mind when you're separated from them, temporarily.

- I know it's very on-brand for a Baptist preacher to write these words, but America has a problem with alcohol. The American Medical Association says alcoholism rose 49% in the first ten years of this century. Today, one in eight American adults is an alcoholic. Aside from the statistics, I see evidence of our alcohol problem every time I go to a sporting event. I never go to a game without seeing multiple people who are drunk to a degree that their sober selves would find embarrassing. But they do it again the next week. In fact, on days the game starts before noon, they complain that it's too early for them to come and tailgate. That tells me two things: A great many of us decided at some point that we can't have a good time sober. And a great many of us aren't aware of just how badly alcohol affects them. That is bondage. That is idolatry.

- The rise of the "social media influencer" over the past ten years is a cultural trend that none of us saw coming. Imagine explaining to a member of the "Greatest Generation" (the Americans who survived the Great Depression and won World War II) what an "influencer" is: "A person who lives such an awesome, fun life, documenting it all in pictures posted online, companies pay them gobs of money to endorse their products." The person from the past might ask, "So, you take their advice about skin care or shoes or exercise equipment because they have proven themselves to be exceptionally wise and moral?" "No," you respond. "We take their advice because we want to live the fantastic lives they do."

Consumerism: As a popular internet meme puts it, "Money can't buy happiness, but it's a heck of a lot more comfortable to cry in a Mercedes than on a bicycle." Or more pointedly, "Anyone who says money can't buy happiness doesn't know where to shop." Most Americans seem convinced that if we feel sad, the solution is as simple as finding a new restaurant, a more stylish outfit, or a fancier Air BnB. This thinking even rears its head in the way Christians think about church. We leave worship on Sundays rating the service the way we would a coffee shop or a concert. We give negative points if the music wasn't our preferred style, or if the sermon didn't keep us engaged. We gaze longingly at the larger church across town with brighter, shinier facilities and cutting edge programs for every member of our family. We focus everything on one question, "What am I getting out of this?" That's ironic, since Scripture is clear that when it comes to corporate worship, God—not us—is the audience. The question we should be asking after every Sunday service is, "What did I contribute?"

Laziness: The book of Proverbs has many warnings for "the sluggard." 26:13-16 is just one example. Most of us would deny laziness as one of our attributes, but just see if any of these satiric descriptions sound like you:

V. 13: *The sluggard says, "There is a lion in the road! There is a lion in the streets!"* The god of comfort makes us fearful. We see dangers everywhere. Whether it's from lone-gunmen mass shooters, disease-spreading microbes, or simply uncomfortable conversations with people we don't like, our fears make it seem safer and more reasonable to do nothing.

V 14: *As a door turns on its hinges, so does a sluggard on his bed.* There's certainly no sin in getting enough sleep. In fact, it can be one of several ways (along with healthy eating and proper exercise) to be a faithful steward of the body you've been given. But today, we've turned "self-care" into a religion all its own, with expensive products, internet gurus, and rituals that promise to make life worth living. How many of us are so invested in nurturing our own temporary body, we never take time to serve others…and lay up treasure for eternity?

V. 15: *The sluggard buries his hand in the dish; it wears him out to bring it back to his mouth.* I'll bet you didn't know Solomon (the author of Proverbs) had a sense of humor. I challenge any stand-up comedian to come up with a more savage, sarcastic takedown of our lousier tendencies than this one. None of us has ever been too lazy to eat. But the Word of God—our true, sustaining feast—sits untasted by most people who claim to be Christians. God has given us a spectacular gift, a book that tells us everything we need to know in order to live a meaningful, joyful life. And it sits there, unconsumed, while we make excuses…then wonder why our souls are so empty.

V. 16: *The sluggard is wiser in his own eyes than seven men who can answer sensibly.* Being a highly opinionated know-it-all is another form of laziness. We love the sound of our own voice, but cannot stand to listen to someone with a different viewpoint. In fact, we shout them down rather than take the time to learn something new. It's just too painful to admit we might be wrong. It's too much work to open our minds to the wisdom that comes from hearing others.

Entitlement: Like the snake-oil salesmen of old, the god of comfort knows how to appeal to our instincts. As Tiffany Matthew writes, "The devil also spreads the lie that we *deserve* to be comfortable and that we can only be happy if we have security and free access to the pleasures of this world. This is why businesses like Netflix and Amazon thrive, because they have the ability to **instantaneously** meet our desires. This is also why the pornography and human trafficking industries continue to flourish, because humans have an insatiable desire to feel good about ourselves and put *our wants above others.*"[xi]

In 2016, when Christian blogger Glennon Doyle announced she was marrying soccer star Abby Wambach, she insisted that God approved of her decision. In fact, she wrote, she had a responsibility to her many Christian readers to model what it was like to be "so comfortable in your own being, your own skin, your own knowing— that you become more interested in your own joy and freedom and integrity than in what others think about you." In an article in Christianity Today, Jen Michel Pollock summed up what Doyle was really saying, and why it was the opposite of discipleship: "In other words, happiness is our only duty today, self-betrayal our only sin. It's not simply that the lines of morality have blurred in modern times, making truth relative. It's not even that religious belief has waned. Rather, the good life has been radically redefined according to the benefit of the individual while the former measures of

63

flourishing—God's glory, society's health, the family's well-being— have been displaced. We're all on the throne now."[vii] When your true god is comfort, you can justify any sin on the rationale that, "God, if He really loves me, would want me to be happy…and this makes me happy."

Tribalism: Comfort idolatry may be the biggest barrier to racial reconciliation and equality in the world. Most of us—no matter our racial background—feel more comfortable being around our own tribe. That means no matter how much we agree with high-minded rhetoric like Martin Luther King's "I Have a Dream" speech in theory, we will usually choose to support the outcome that benefits "my people" over bringing people together. That's true in the church, as well as the wider world. Though I almost never encounter overt racism in Christians I worship alongside, I often see how the god of comfort keeps us safely ensconced among our own tribe.

Many years ago, the church I pastored had an opportunity to merge with a smaller church made up of Spanish-speakers. To me, it was an idea that made sense; we were living in a community that was majority Latino, and we were a mostly Anglo church. Being able to offer a worship service and Bible studies in Spanish would enable us to reach people we weren't currently able to reach with the Gospel. Obviously, this was a big decision, so we held a meeting for all church members to ask questions, raise concerns, and help us decide whether to proceed. The meeting became very emotionally charged. Most members seemed to be against the idea. Some expressed fears that this Spanish-speaking group would outgrow us, and then take over "our" church. A minority answered back that we should do whatever was necessary for the spread of the Gospel. One woman summed up the feelings of many when she said, "I've been a member of this church for years, and I keep coming here even though I no longer live in this neighborhood. But if the day comes that it doesn't feel like my church anymore, I will just find a church closer to me." I knew these people well. They were my friends. I can tell you for a fact that they weren't racists. They had been kind and welcoming whenever individuals or families of Hispanic background joined our church. Many had Latino family members. But in their lifetimes, they had seen everything about their community change. Meat markets had become carnicerias; billboards in Spanish were at least as common as those in English. Their church was the only thing that still seemed the same; the one place that was still "ours." In the end, that desire to maintain a comfortable place—instead of anything having to do with the Gospel--was the deciding factor.

Slaying the Snake

So how do we defeat the idol of comfort in our lives? The Bible shows us the way.

Practice self-denial. Jesus' famous invitation was, *If anyone would come after me, let him deny himself, take up his cross daily and follow me.* We live in a time so affluent, we can have virtually anything we want in an instant. Want to see a blockbuster movie or live sporting event? Just stream it from the comfort of your living room (or on your smartphone). Want some jewelry, furniture, or clothes? Amazon can get it to you by tomorrow…if not sooner. Craving some Greek food, or barbecue, or tacos? You can have it delivered in an hour or less. So why would we intentionally deny ourselves any of it? Well, think about it this way: A hot fudge sundae is a good thing. So is a lazy day at home. But if my goal is to lose weight and get in shape, too much of either one is a very bad thing. I have to deny myself in order to reach my goal. As disciples of Jesus, our goal is to love God and love others. That is the life that brings joy and purpose, and that impacts eternity. In order to get there, we carve out time to meditate on Scripture, pray and serve. That means we get up earlier than we otherwise would; we spend less time on our hobbies than we want; we get out of our comfort zone (interesting term, isn't it?) so that we can get our hands dirty helping people who have less than we do. But it's worth it.

One of the more famous verses in the Bible is Philippians 4:13,

I can do all things through Christ who strengthens me. People take that verse out of context to say, "I can accomplish anything I set my mind to." No, that's not what it means. Paul is writing from a prison cell. He is telling his friends, "I've lost all my freedom, and I may be executed tomorrow, but don't worry. I'm doing great." How can he have joy in the midst of that kind of pain? He writes just before that, *I have learned in whatever situation I am to be content. I know how to be brought low, and I know how to abound. In any and every circumstance, I have learned the secret of facing plenty and hunger, abundance and need.* Paul learned how to be content through denying himself. He learned that God gave him enough joy that he wouldn't miss those things too badly when they were taken away. So is your life a constant quest to get more of what you want? Or do you intentionally deny yourself some things for the purpose of growing in Christ?

Don't waste your pain. James 1:2-4 says, *Count it all joy, my brothers, when you meet trials of various kinds, for you know that the testing of your faith produces steadfastness. And let steadfastness have its full effect, that you may be perfect and complete, lacking in nothing.* This doesn't mean we should go looking for trouble, or inflict pain on ourselves on purpose. But when trials come, we recognize that God's plan is not defeated by them. We rejoice in knowing He can use them in our lives to do amazing things.

So, for instance: You find out that the debilitating pain you are experiencing is incurable; it won't get better. The industry you've trained for and worked in your entire life dries up financially, and you're nowhere near ready to retire. Your child is diagnosed with a serious mental illness. You suffer a miscarriage. The person you thought was the love of your life breaks off the engagement. All of these are terrible things. As a Christian, you ask God to take the pain away, to work a miracle. But don't stop there. Ask Him to help you see what He's doing in the midst of your pain. It could be that this is a moment in your life when your relationship with Him grows more than ever before. Maybe this is when your church family rallies around you, and a revival breaks out in your heart and theirs. This could be a moment when God equips you to help people who in the future will experience exactly what you're going through right now. So rejoice. God loves you. Like a good parent, He grieves alongside you. He does not enjoy watching you struggle. If you'll let Him, He will make this a life-changing moment. So muster up the courage and faith to pray, "Lord, please make this pain go away. But until you do, please don't let me miss what you're trying to do in my life through this."

Live in hope. A few years ago, a friend of mine was diagnosed with ALS. He was young, with loving wife and a beautiful little girl. A few years later, he passed away, and I did the funeral. I felt led to preach on 2 Corinthians 4:17-18, *For this light momentary affliction is preparing for us an eternal weight of glory beyond all comparison, as we look not to the things that are seen but to the things that are unseen.* I really doubted myself. Could I really call my friend's afflictions light and momentary? I realized I couldn't...unless Heaven is real. There is nothing light about realizing you won't see your daughter grow up, or slowly losing your ability to walk, then talk, then swallow, then breathe...while you're still in your thirties. But if Heaven is real, then for all eternity those years of pain will seem like a bad dream he can barely remember. The next time we see him, he'll be running, jumping, climbing, eating, laughing...and we will too.

Hope is knowing that something better is coming. Hope can enable us to handle any kind of pain without being overwhelmed. When our first child was being born, I was more scared than my wife, Carrie, was. I had seen too many movies in which the woman in labor levitates, her head spinning around as she screams profanities at her husband. I was begging the doctor to give her an epidural almost as soon as we got there. But Carrie, on the other hand, was gracious and calm. She knew that it was going to be painful, but at the end, there was something wonderful coming. And so for my friend; even on the worst day of his life, the day he received his fatal diagnosis, he could say, "Yes, and now I'm one day closer to being where I've always wanted to be." The idol of comfort says, "Life is short. This world is as good as it gets. Find pleasure wherever you can, before it's too late." Don't believe that lie. It will break your heart and lead you to make terrible decisions. Instead, pray, "Lord, teach me to walk in hope, to think about the New Earth every single day. Help me live with one eye on the life to come."

Find your joy and comfort in God. Comfort idolatry is snake oil. It makes grand promises: Buy this. Achieve that. Join our team. Follow this plan, and you'll have a pain-free life. But God is the real thing. Psalm 16:11 says it this way: *You make known to me the path of life; in your presence there is fullness of joy; at your right hand are pleasures forevermore*. Again, it's not that it's wrong to enjoy the little pleasures life brings: A great meal, a bucket list vacation, a night out with some good friends, a holiday with your entire family, buying something you've always wanted, becoming really good at your favorite sport. But you recognize none of those things lasts forever. Your life isn't built around those experiences. The point of your life is knowing God and serving Him. He is your source of joy and comfort, and He will never leave you or forsake you. CS Lewis said "Don't let your happiness depend on something you could lose." When your life is wrapped up in knowing and loving God above all things, your highest good is something you can't possibly lose. So any anger or anxiety or sorrow you feel is only temporary; it doesn't destroy or overwhelm you. This only happens when we crown God as King of our lives, and when we maintain the spiritual disciplines—studying Scripture, prayer, corporate worship—that keep us in constant contact with Him.

There once was a woman who suffered with a chronic illness for twelve years. This illness rendered her ritually unclean; she was unable to worship in the Jewish temple, and ordinary relationships with people were almost impossible. She went to doctors, but they turned out to be snake oil salesmen. So she was in pain, absolutely alone, and now she was broke as well. One day, she heard that Jesus was passing through her town. She ran to the sound of voices. She had no idea what would happen. Maybe He was just a snake oil salesman too. Maybe He would turn her away, like everyone else had. She forced her way through the throngs of people pressing up against this man. People yelled at her as she brushed past them, but she didn't care. If this didn't work, she was done.

Finally, she got to Him. She chose not to speak, just in case He would reject her. She leaned forward until she was prone to the ground and reached as far ahead as she could...and touched the edge of His tunic. Instantly, she felt an amazing sensation. She couldn't say how, but she knew she was healed. Then she noticed He had stopped walking. "Who touched me?" He asked. Her heart stopped. As He turned around, He saw her there, still lying face down. Afraid to even lift her face, she said, "I touched you, Lord." Here was a woman who didn't understand that what she had been looking for her whole life, what she had thrown all her money away to obtain, was actually free of charge. She didn't know that God was on her side, so much so He had come to lay down His life for her sins. She looked up and saw a face full of more kindness and love than she ever dared to dream. "Go in peace," He said, "your faith has saved you." (Luke 8:43-48) Friend, what are you reaching out for today? What are you praying for? Your God has what you need, and He loves to give it away. Will you pray, "Lord, teach me to enjoy the blessings you give, but to find my joy and comfort only in you"?

Chapter 6

You Really Like Me: The Idol of Approval

In 1984, Sally Field won the Academy Award for best actress for her role in Places in the Heart (If you've never seen the movie, find it. Watch it. It's one of my all-time favorites). She stepped to the podium and delivered one of the most famous lines in Hollywood history: "I haven't had an orthodox career, and I've wanted more than anything to have your respect. The first time I didn't feel it, but this time I feel it, and I can't deny the fact that you like me, right now, you like me!" She wasn't talking to the general public; she was talking to her peers, her fellow actors. She was aware that she was seen as something less than a serious actress. She was known for roles like Gidget, The Flying Nun, and Burt Reynolds' love interest in Smokey and the Bandit. Not exactly Meryl Streep territory. But now she had won Best Actress for a second time. Now she truly felt respected and accepted. People love to make fun of that speech; they usually misquote it as, "You like me, you really like me!" But Sally Field was just expressing what most of us feel in one way or another. In one research study, participants were given letters written to them by important people in their lives, letters in which these people expressed admiration for some quality they saw in them. The participants were put into MRI machines, so their brains could be studied as they read these letters. What the MRI showed was that the brain experiences that kind of affirmation as intense pleasure, similar to what happens when we eat a bowl of our favorite ice cream. We love to feel accepted, admired, affirmed. And to have that acceptance taken away can feel worse than death.

People have always been like this. Two thousand years ago,

Jesus came into our world. Everyone who met Him was confronted with a stark choice: Faced with God in the flesh, would they repent and change the trajectory of their lives forever? Or would they reject what they saw in Jesus and cling to their current path? The religious elites of the time for the most part rejected Him, because they had the most to lose. If Jesus was truly God, then much of what they believed about who God was and how He wants us to live was wrong. Yet in John 12:42-43 we read this poignant detail: *Nevertheless, many even of the authorities believed in him, but for fear of the Pharisees they did not confess it, so that they would not be put out of the synagogue; for they loved the glory that comes from man more than the glory that comes from God.* Jesus has just entered Jerusalem on a donkey, just days before He would face the cross. The crowds loudly praised Him. They quoted Old Testament verses about the promised Messiah. But the religious leaders of Israel criticized the people for this. Some of these leaders really did believe that Jesus was the Son of God, but they held back from following Him because of what their peers might think. Tragically, their need for approval kept them from experiencing salvation. Of course, we live in a very different time. Most of us don't have to sacrifice the approval of people we respect in order to be baptized. But approval addiction is still something that can be devastating to our walk with Christ and our ability to live out God's purpose in life.

The Roar of the Crowd

In my opinion, there are two different ways approval addiction manifests itself in our lives. One is a need for applause and attention. Someone once said of Teddy Roosevelt, "He wants to be the bride at every wedding and the corpse at every funeral." Some of us are not far from that. We're happiest when people are focused on us: hanging on every word of one of our stories, laughing at a quick-witted comment we just made, or congratulating us on our latest accomplishment. Almost everyone appreciates positive feedback, but approval addicts yearn for it like oxygen. This longing for praise can drive us to do things we might never have thought ourselves capable of doing.

Barry Bonds is, by almost any metric, the greatest baseball player in history. He holds two of the most hallowed records in the game: Most home runs in a season, and most home runs in a career. Yet he may never be elected to the baseball Hall of Fame, because of his well-documented use of performance-enhancing drugs. Ironically, Bonds was easily one of baseball's all-time greats even before he started taking steroids. He was that rarest of jewels, a true "five tool player," (baseball jargon for someone who can run, throw, field, hit for average and for power). By 1998, he was 34 years old and had already secured his place in baseball lore. This was the height of baseball's steroid era, when dozens (or perhaps even hundreds) of players were "juicing."

It's not difficult to understand what led these athletes to pursue an illegal—and potentially harmful—course. Imagine knowing that there was a substance that would enable you to run just a bit faster, throw a little harder, hit the ball a tad further. Now imagine that small boost was all you needed to be able to make it to the major leagues, where contracts—even for a role player—are so large, you and your family will be set for life. Now imagine that you know many other players who are getting into the majors ahead of you, because they're using this substance. Or imagine you are a long-time player whose skills are starting to slip, and you believe steroids can keep you playing for several more years. Bonds, however, was no minor leaguer hoping to break into the big leagues. Nor was he an old-timer trying to hang on to the game. So why did he do it?

In 1998, the season before Bonds started using steroids, two other players, Mark McGwire and Sammy Sosa, captivated the nation with an epic season-long duel to see who would be first to break baseball's record for most home runs in a season. Before one game between Bonds' San Francisco Giants and McGwire's St Louis Cardinals, Bonds was reportedly furious to see so many people turn out to watch McGwire take pre-game batting practice. Bonds knew that McGwire and Sosa were almost certainly using steroids. The next season, when Bonds showed up for training camp, his body had been transformed from lean and athletic to grotesquely muscular. In short, Barry Bonds ruined his legacy and damaged his health because he envied the attention that other players were getting. Being a great player alone was not enough; He had to be number one in the eyes of the fans.

Please understand: competitiveness and a drive to be successful are not inherently sinful qualities. When they are harnessed by the Spirit of Christ, they can become powerful tools for good, in fact. For that matter, if you enjoy receiving compliments or being the center of attention, that doesn't mean you are less righteous than someone who is more private and introverted. That is simply your personality type. But those of us who have this trait should remember the Lord's words in Mark 8:36, *For what does it profit a man to gain the whole world and forfeit his soul?* History is littered with the names of men and women who gave their lives to achieve the world's acclaim, and ended in emptiness. One more Barry Bonds story: During the peak of his muscle-bound glory, when his hitting prowess was universally feared, and everyone knew he was "juicing," his San Francisco Giants played the Astros in Houston. During his first at-bat, the Astros pitcher intentionally hit Bonds. In response, the crowd gave the pitcher a standing ovation. Barry Bonds wanted applause, and he got it…only not in the way he hoped. That is the inevitable end of approval addiction.

I Want You to Want Me

There is another form of approval addiction, and this one afflicts more than just extreme extroverts, would-be celebrities, and sore losers. People with more reserved personalities are just as likely to be addicted. For them, this idolatry manifests as an unspoken creed: "My life only has meaning and I only have worth if _____ loves and respects me." What name would you put in that blank? Perhaps it's a romantic interest. How many of us have experienced a breakup or rejection that devastated us to the point of despair…even suicidal thoughts? When we look back at those relationships from a distance of several years, we can't believe how we allowed this one person's acceptance to control us. But that is the power of idolatry. Perhaps you're a parent, and you would put the names of your children in that blank; or perhaps it's your spouse whose opinion matters most. Maybe you're still desperately trying to win the approval of a mother or father. We'll talk more about this when we get to our chapter on family as idolatry, but for now I'll simply say this: In every relationship, there is heartache. You irritate them; they disappoint you. That's hard enough in a healthy relationship, but when it rises to the level of worship, that broken heart can never heal.

For some of us, the name in that blank would be the name of a group, not an individual. Many working people strive for the respect of their co-workers. Some academics need to be seen by their colleagues as smart and enlightened. Often women are paralyzed by the things their female acquaintances might say about their clothes, their weight, their hair, or how their kids behave; and often men put on a constant, exhausting show of inflated toughness and masculinity so that their buddies don't think they're "soft." Religious people can be obsessed with their reputation within the church, while many others conform their every opinion and lifestyle choice to fit neatly within their political party, ethnic group, or circle of friends. To face their rejection—or even criticism—is a possibility so anxiety-inducing, we don't even want to imagine it. If we're honest, many of us would put the word "everyone" in that blank. We cannot live with ourselves if we know someone is angry with us. Insults and mockery hit us deep; we can't stand feeling like a laughing stock in the sight of others. Even the harsh words of a distant acquaintance, someone we don't even like, or a total stranger can send us into a tailspin.

None of us is completely impervious to the feelings of others, nor should we be. We were made by God with a need for human affection. When our relationships are broken, or when we've hurt people God gave us to love, we should care deeply about it. And the Bible talks about the importance of having a good reputation (Proverbs 22:1, Ecclesiastes 7:1). One of the reasons the first Christians spread the Gospel so well is that they "had the favor of all the people" (Acts 2:47). But when your desire to impress people outweighs your desire to know and glorify God, it can lead to terrible decisions. Teenagers do wildly foolish, even permanently life-altering things to impress their friends (more on that later). Tough but needed conversations are avoided, because we'd rather not risk making the other person angry. Relationships that should be loving become possessive, controlling, smothering. Christians drift away from the Gospel and into rigid legalism to impress the rest of the "frozen chosen." We gossip about, ostracize, or ridicule others, because it deflects the scorn of our group onto someone else, and makes us look good by comparison. Meanwhile, we live with the constant, churning

74

stress of what might happen if we lose that approval.

And then there are those privileged individuals who fit both categories. These souls need both applause and assurance. I must confess I fit that description. Out of all the idols in the world, this is the one I struggle with the most. When I was in fourth grade, I read a poem my teacher chose for me in an academic competition against kids from towns all over our region. When it was announced that I had won first place in Oral Reading, my entire school erupted in applause. That felt awfully good. I wanted to do whatever I could to make that happen again...and again. Decades later, every Sunday, I get up to preach the Word of God to a group of people, knowing that my idolatry is craving their approval. Every Sunday, I must pray for the Holy Spirit to search my heart and show me if I am motivated by a desire to get human applause or to glorify God.

At the same time, I struggle from the quieter version of approval addiction too: Deep down inside, I want everyone to be happy with me all the time. There is a difference between being nice and being kind. Niceness is a fine attribute that makes the world more pleasant, but it's not a fruit of the Spirit (Galatians 5:22-23), like kindness. Niceness is a second-rate virtue. It's being polite enough not to offend anyone, without caring enough to actually help them. It's focused on gaining and keeping the approval of others by adhering to the codes of society, when we should be focused on the will of God. Niceness, in other words, is all about how others think of me. But kindness is about you. It's putting myself in your shoes and doing what I would want someone to do for me in that situation. Kindness is sacrificial. It doesn't always feel nice. For instance, sometimes the kind thing to do is to say something that you might find offensive. I find it easy to be nice; that's the way I was raised, and it feeds my need for approval. But I am praying that God would make me truly kind.

Can you imagine if Jesus had been motivated by approval? He would have withered in the face of the criticism His enemies heaped upon Him. Or He would have preached what people wanted to hear in order to increase the size of His crowds. Instead, He was condemned, insulted, and falsely accused on a daily basis, without ever responding to their disrespect with anger or self-pity. He often did or said things that seemed custom-designed to make people think twice about following Him, which is the opposite of every other preacher I know (including me). Jesus was a human being with feelings like ours; how could He be so impervious to the fickle feelings of people? I believe it's because He knew whose approval truly mattered. On two separate occasions--At the river Jordan after His baptism and on top of Mount Hermon during His transfiguration--Jesus heard a voice from Heaven saying, "This is my Son, whom I love. Listen to Him." It's as if God the Father said to His Son, "This is a tough world you're in. No matter what happens, just know that I love you." For Jesus, the applause of Heaven was the only applause He sought; the approval of His Father was the only approval He needed.

Symptoms of Approval Addiction

You may be thinking, "That's all fine, Jeff. But this is not something I struggle with." Don't be so sure. Approval is a deep idol. Some idols are embedded so deep in us, like power, comfort and approval, they can manifest in a wide variety of ways. That means your addiction to approval might look very different from mine. So let's run through some symptoms of approval addiction. Like the symptoms of a disease, none of us will have all of these signs; but most of us will have some of them. When you read one that might be true of you, circle it. By the way, now is the time to be radically honest with yourself.

I can't say no, so I overcommit instead of risking disappointing someone.

I am afraid to risk failure or embarrassment. This is one reason (although not the only one) why so many of us are terrified to speak in public. It's why many of us never volunteer to serve God in a new way. We can't risk the possibility of looking foolish, or feeling like we didn't do well.

I am two-faced. Rather than lovingly confront someone about flaws they need to address, I choose to talk about them behind their back. I get to feel self-righteous without all the awkwardness.

It bothers me terribly to have anyone angry with me. I'll lose sleep trying to think of what I might have done to get on their bad side, and strategizing ways to win them over again.

Criticism sticks with me; I get defensive or angry when someone points out things I need to improve. Have you heard the saying, "If one hundred people complement you and one criticizes you, you'll remember the one"? That's a sign of approval addiction.

I am overly concerned with appearance; I dress to be noticed. There's nothing wrong with looking your best. But what is your motivation? Here's a way to measure this: When you see a group picture that you're in, do you mostly focus on how you look in that picture? Here's another: Do you spend more time working on your outward appearance than you do on your inner character?

I get resentful when someone else is praised, when their idea gets noticed, or their joke gets laughed at. If you've ever said, "I don't see why everyone seems to think _____ is so great," that's what we might call approval envy. You feel that their glory diminishes you.

I avoid tough conversations. Proverbs 27:6 says, *Faithful are the wounds of a friend.* How often do you "faithfully wound" your friends by speaking the truth to them in love? Do you ever confront people who are making terrible choices? Do you speak about your faith to co-workers and neighbors who aren't believers?

I often say I don't care what others think of me. Here's the ultimate irony. I've known plenty of people who were eager to tell me that they didn't care one bit what anyone thought of them. Meanwhile, all I can wonder is, "Why are you telling me this? Are you trying to impress me?" That's image management, which is a form of approval addiction too.

We started this chapter by looking at the religious leaders of Israel, who cared so much about their reputation, they missed God's Messiah. They loved the glory that comes from man more than the glory that comes from God. Paul was a student of those men. There was a time when he very much lived to please others. He was on the fast track to greatness within Judaism. As he says in Philippians 3, he was a Hebrew of Hebrews, a law-abiding Pharisee. To impress his leaders and peers, he went so far as to persecute the Church. When Paul became a Christian, that applause and approval were gone. The first time he preached the Gospel, in Damascus, his own people tried to kill him. He went to meet the apostles in Jerusalem, and at first, they rejected him too. For the rest of his life, he would face everything from gossip behind his back to lynch mobs. Paul writes in Galatians 1:10, *For am I now seeking the approval of man, or of God? Or am I trying to please man? If I were still trying to please man, I would not be a servant of Christ.* The Galatians had criticized him, implying he wasn't a real apostle since he hadn't followed Jesus during our Lord's earthly lifetime. Paul shows us the choice he has to make: "I can't be led by my desire to impress you, to win your approval. If that's what is motivating me, I'm no longer serving Christ. And I choose to serve Christ, even if you reject me for it."

But in case you think Paul was an insensitive man who didn't care a whit what others thought, you need to read 1 Corinthians 9:19-22: *For though I am free from all, I have made myself a servant to all, that I might win more of them. To the Jews I became as a Jew, in order to win Jews. To those under the law I became as one under the law (though not being myself under the law) that I might win those under the law. To those outside the law I became as one outside the law (not being outside the law of God but under the law of Christ) that I might win those outside the law. To the weak I became weak, that I might win the weak. I have become all things to all people, that by all means I might save some.* Paul still cared intensely about the thoughts and feelings of others. The difference between the old, approval-addicted Paul and the new one was that he was motivated by what people thought about Jesus because of his life and words; He wasn't motivated by what they thought of him.

Take a look at the symptoms of approval addiction you've circled. Think about how different they would look if you truly cared only about what people thought of Jesus because of your life. In fact, write what you wish those statements about you said instead. It might read something like this:

I know I can't please everyone all the time, and I'm fine with that, as long as I see evidence I'm influencing people toward Jesus.

I tell people the truth in a loving way, even if it's not what they want to hear.

I try to look my best, but I spend way more time improving my character than my appearance.

When people are angry with me, I do everything I can to be reconciled. If they refuse, I rest in the knowledge that my Father accepts me.

When I am criticized, I am thankful for the chance to learn and grow. When the criticism is inaccurate and unfair, I rejoice. That's how people treated my Lord, after all.

When someone else is in the spotlight, I am genuinely happy for them. When the spotlight turns to me, my top priority is to represent Christ well.

I have nothing to hide, nothing to be ashamed of. I never pretend to be anything that I am not. I love who I am in Christ.

Approval Addicts Anonymous

So now that you've seen where you want to go, how do you get there? The same way Paul did. It was a face-to-face meeting with Jesus that made all the difference (see the story in Acts 9). One moment he was on his way to Damascus to arrest Christians, hoping that would impress his superiors and validate him. His approval addiction had made him arrogant, self-righteous, and hateful. The next moment he was willing to face criticism, prison and martyrdom with joy in his heart. Jesus made the difference. You can't break approval addiction on your own. It just won't work. But take it to Jesus. Confess the specific ways approval addiction affects you. Tell Him, "Lord, I am tired of letting my need for approval rule my life, steal my joy, and keep me from truly loving people. Today, I choose to please you above all others. Give me the strength to follow that through." Pray the same thing the next day…and the next day…until He takes you home.

It was the last week of my senior year of high school. I was standing in the hallway with my friend Chris; I can't remember why we weren't in class. A girl walked by us. I had briefly dated this girl. She said something mildly sarcastic to me, then walked into the girls' bathroom. Chris said, "Are you going to take that from her?" Chris wasn't just my friend. He was the coolest guy I knew. He was tall and movie-star handsome, a fantastic athlete, and very popular with girls....none of which were qualities I possessed. I desperately wanted to impress him. So when he asked, "Are you going to take that from her?" I indignantly said, "No!" And I threw open the door of the girls' bathroom just to make him laugh. The girl was standing at the mirror; she looked at me with a shocked expression. It was then that I realized I hadn't really thought this plan through. I turned to leave, and found myself face to face with a teacher. She said, "Come with me," and took me to the principal's office. Chris was really laughing now, but I wasn't.

Our principal, Mr. Manning, was a local legend. He had led our football team to the state championship game in the 1950s, the only time our little town had gone that far. He had later coached my own father and uncles. There I sat in Mr. Manning's office, shaking like a leaf as the teacher told him what I had done. I was never the sort of kid who got into trouble, so I had no idea what was about to happen to me. Remember, this was the last week of my senior year. What if they didn't let me walk in the graduation ceremony that weekend? What if they held me back a year? Mr. Manning waited judiciously for the teacher to leave his office, then he burst out laughing. I was too shocked at this unexpected turn of events to laugh along with him. Finally, he composed himself. "Berger," he said, "I think you've learned your lesson, haven't you?" I assured him I had, and he set me free. It was a moment of unexpected grace. And it makes me think...someday, we'll all stand before a much higher authority than a high school principal. We'll think of all those foolish things we did, said and thought to impress others, and wish we had acted differently. But the best news of all is that God's grace is even greater than the grace I received that day. We are accepted in the only place that ultimately matters because He came to earth and took our rejection upon Himself. He was despised so we could be loved. He was crucified so we could live forever. He loves you. He really, really loves you.

Chapter 7

It Starts at Home: The Idol of Family

This chapter might be the hardest one for many of us, because we're used to seeing family as an unquestioned, ultimate good. But remember our definition of an idol: It's anything that does for you what only God should do: It gives you security, identity, purpose and happiness. It demands your absolute obedience and allegiance. If there is anything in your life that you think you simply couldn't live without, it's an idol. You might say, "By that definition, sure, my family is an idol. But I still don't see how it's a bad thing to love them too much. If I lose sleep over them, I'm just hurting myself to benefit the ones I love." I would argue that that's not the case at all, actually. In fact, the ultimate irony of family idolatry is that it doesn't just hurt us by separating us from God; it actually hurts them, too.

But first, let's make something clear: The Bible is a very pro-family book, because God is a pro-family God. In the second chapter of the Bible, long before there was a Church or a State, we see this:

Therefore a man shall leave his father and his mother and hold fast to his wife, and they shall become one flesh (Genesis 2:24).

In Exodus, God prepares a group of former slaves to build a new nation. They will be Israel, the people chosen to be priests to the nations, drawing others to God's salvation by the glowing example of their righteousness. At Mount Sinai, when God gave to Moses the Ten Commandments, it was similar to our American Bill of Rights. It was the founding principles of their new nation. The importance of the family made up one-fifth of the list. As you might know, Commandment number five is:

Honor your father and your mother, that your days may be long in the land that the LORD your God is giving you (Exodus 20:12).

Notice the promise at the end of that verse. The "you" is plural (a better translation would be, "that the Lord is giving y'all," but apparently not enough Hebrew scholars are from the American South). He wasn't saying that any child who honors his parents will have a long life. He was telling Israel collectively that their nation would last forever in the land if they built strong families. In other words, God is telling us that a strong, stable society is built on solid families.

Commandment number seven goes on to ban adultery. Again, God is founding this new nation on the principle that strong families create and sustain a strong society. He's saying, "Don't wreck someone's family by stealing their spouse." In ancient Israel, both of those commandments were punishable by death.

Jesus came along at a time when Jewish men thought it was fine to divorce your wife for any reason at all (of course, wives didn't have the same rights), but Jesus said men should stay with their wives until death (Matthew 19:1-9). Paul went even further, saying a man should lay down his life for his wife (Ephesians 5:25). In a world where women were seen as the property of their husbands, this was revolutionary. God was saying, "I hold you men accountable for how you treat your wives. If you mistreat one of my daughters, you'll answer to me." On the other hand, Paul's command to wives to be submissive (Ephesians 5:22-24) is often seen today as regressive. But, again, women in that culture had no rights to begin with. Submission was their lot in life. So the question we should ask is, "Why did Paul feel the need to command wives to do what society already expected them to do?" The answer is that, when Christianity began to spread, with its revolutionary ideas about being born again to new life, and everyone being equal at the foot of the cross, there was a danger that wives who had converted would then say, "I'm not the woman who married this man. I'm someone new. I should leave him so that I can serve Jesus wholeheartedly." Paul's point was that a woman's Christian faith should make her more loyal to her husband, not less. Loving him is the same as obeying Christ. Think of it: A husband who consistently sacrifices His own desires and preferences to serve His wife, helping her be all she was meant to be in Christ, while at the same time that wife works joyfully to build up her husband and meet his needs as if she's blessing Jesus Himself. It seems to me that's the kind of marriage we all want.

But of course, there's more where that came from. As we've already seen, there are numerous Scriptures extolling the beauty of a passionate love between husband and wife. Not only did God invent marriage, He literally wrote the book on it. And then there are the multitudes of passages about children and parenting. For instance, Psalms 127 tells us that children are to be treasured:

Behold, children are a heritage from the LORD, the fruit of the womb a reward. Like arrows in the hand of a warrior are the children of one's youth. Blessed is the man who fills his quiver with them! He shall not be put to shame when he speaks with his enemies in the gate. Psalm 127:3-5

In Deuteronomy 6, Moses put the responsibility for passing the faith of Israel to the next generation in the hands of the parents, not the priests:

And these words that I command you today shall be on your heart. You shall teach them diligently to your children, and shall talk of them when you sit in your house, and when you walk by the way, and when you lie down, and when you rise. You shall bind them as a sign on your hand, and they shall be as frontlets between your eyes. Deuteronomy 6:6-7

The Greco-Roman world of Jesus' lifetime could be a brutal

place for children. Philosophers held a certain contempt for childhood as a phase of human life. Of course, many Gentile parents loved their children, but no one seemed to object to practices such as exposure of unwanted infants, abortion, and the forced prostitution of both boys and girls. Jewish culture, with the heritage of Moses' law, was a kinder place for kids, but still didn't see them as an integral part of community life. Along came Jesus, telling His disciples that they needed to become like a little child to enter the Kingdom of God, commanding them to "let the children come unto me," and teaching them to call God "Father" (the Hebrew word "Abba," which even a little child could say). Scholar O. M. Bakke's book title says it all: *When Children Became People: The Birth of Childhood in Early Christianity.* Bakke's thesis is that our modern idea of childhood as a crucial time of development, and of children as priceless treasures that our society should protect and invest in, was non-existent before Jesus. He changed everything.

The sanctity of marriage and the importance of children were foundational principles of the Christian faith, and they radically changed the world. As Western culture spread, those values spread with them, and strengthened countries like ours. Even if we never perfectly lived up to those ideals, we held them up as the standard. We aspired to them. And it made us who we are.

That all started to change in the middle of the last century, with the Sexual Revolution in our country. American culture started to celebrate unhindered sexual expression as an absolute right; all the old standards and mores were seen to be oppressive. As Christians saw an increase in divorce, cohabitation, single parenting, and a change in the way society talked and thought about marriage and family, the Church's response was to hold up the family unit as the highest of all possible goods. In our quest to counter what we saw as society's attack on the family unit, we've elevated the family to a place it doesn't belong. As one unfortunate by-product of our emphasis on family, many single adults feel out of place in church; Small groups and activities all are structured toward married people with kids, and the singles feel unwanted. To add insult to injury, all of our emphasis on family ministry hasn't stopped divorce rates from rising, and kids from leaving organized Christianity when they grow up. Could it be that, in spite of our best efforts, we've hurt families instead of strengthening them?

The Harsh Words of Jesus

Imagine your church posted this statement on its website: "Our mission is to turn fathers against their sons, and daughters against their mothers." Imagine if, before anyone joined your church, the pastor had a personal conversation with every one saying, "If I find out you love your parents, your spouse or your kids too much, I will personally kick you out of this church." You would be appalled (and would probably look for a new church). But consider the words of Jesus:

Do not think that I have come to bring peace to the earth. I have not come to bring peace, but a sword. For I have come to set a man against his father, and a daughter against her mother, and a daughter-in-law against her mother-in-law. And a person's enemies will be those of his own household. Whoever loves father or mother more than me is not worthy of me, and whoever loves son or daughter more than me is not worthy of me. And whoever does not take his cross and follow me is not worthy of me. Whoever finds his life will lose it, and whoever loses his life for my sake will find it. Matthew 10:34-39

Keep in mind, He was saying these things to a culture that was even more pro-family than American Evangelicalism. Here's what I mean: In our world, when a child chooses some slight rebellion, like dying her hair pink or choosing a career field her parents don't approve of, we say, "Kids have to find their own way." But in ancient Israel (and in many cultures today), a person's individual identity was less important than their devotion to their family. A child who dishonored or displeased his family was seen by society as an inherently bad person, not someone who was figuring out life on his own terms. Most people in that world would rather die than disappoint their families.

85

So why would Jesus say these things? Because even though He created the family, and He loved the family, He didn't want us to put our families before Him. He knows the damage that causes. He chose His words precisely, to help His disciples (and other potential followers) know that they had to reject family idolatry in order to serve alongside Him. His words reveal some of the dangers of idolizing our families:

Family idolatry keeps us from obeying God. We know the stories about how Jesus called people to follow Him. He stands in Peter's boat and says, "Follow me, and I'll teach you to fish for people," and Peter and Andrew, James and John leave their nets in their boats and walk away. He summons Matthew, who has a highly lucrative job as a tax collector, and Matthew quits that very day. But we don't think about what that did to their families. James and John were sons of a man named Zebedee. He ran a business that was essentially "Zebedee and Sons Fishing Co," and I'm sure he was excited about leaving that business to them when he was gone. Now they had thrown that away for some homeless preacher. Paul writes in 1 Corinthians 9:5 that most if not all of the other apostles were married. Who was providing for Peter's wife and kids after he quit fishing? What happened to Matthew's wife and kids, who were probably used to a swanky lifestyle, when he started following Jesus?

For at least three years, these men weren't providing for their families in the way that men were expected to do. Jesus made them choose: Will you do what is expected as family men, or will you obey me? That's why Jesus said He would turn sons against fathers and daughters against mothers. This passage is part of His instructions to the Twelve when He's sending them out to preach and minister on their own for the first time. He's telling them that some of them are going to get pressure from their families. The folks back home are already hearing from the religious leaders that Jesus is a false Messiah and possibly demon-possessed. Now, the disciples will hear from home, "Hey Bartholomew, come back here. Your mother can't show her face in the synagogue." "Thomas, your kids barely have enough to eat. You should be working, providing. Instead, you're acting like a preacher?" "Matthew, when you said you thought Jesus was the Messiah, you didn't tell me that the kids and I would lose the house and have to move back in with my parents!" If you were a member of the Twelve, and your highest value was to put family first, you couldn't obey Jesus.

In Italy in the Middle Ages, a young man from a very wealthy family came to believe that God wanted him to help the poor. So he started giving his fortune away to the less fortunate. His father actually sued this man to stop him. In court, the son literally took off all his clothes, handed them to his dad and said, "I don't need your money anymore. I'm serving my Heavenly Father from now on." We know that man as Francis of Assisi today. We read stories today of people from other religious backgrounds who choose to follow Christ, even though they will be disowned by their families. And perhaps a few of you experienced that when you came to Christ. But for the most part, in our context, our families don't tend to stand between us and Jesus, forcing us to choose one or the other. Instead, our idolatry to family causes disobedience in a more subtle way.

Years ago, I did a funeral of a young woman who passed away, leaving a husband and two preteen kids. I kept up with the husband afterward. They had been churchgoers before, but now we rarely saw them. He wasn't mad at us. He explained, every time we talked, that he intended to get back into church, but now his priority was to spend time with his kids. He said "It's just me now. I have to make sure they know I love them." So he would take them fishing at the lake, or to see Grandparents, or to theme parks. I was there several more years, and they never came back. Please understand: I know going to church isn't the sum total of what it means to follow Christ. In fact, you can be in church every Sunday and be a terrible disciple. But I see us make similar calculations when it comes to family time. We have such busy schedules, and we have to cut something to spend time with our kids. It seems our time with God and our opportunities to serve Him are always first to go. I will sometimes hear a parent say, "My family is my mission field." Amen. No one has more opportunity to reach your spouse and children than you do. But they aren't your only mission field. Can you imagine if when Jesus said, "Follow me and I will teach you to fish for people," Peter had said, "Oh no, Lord, my family is my mission field?" When we use our love of family to excuse our disobedience to God's call, that's idolatry. We worship what we obey, and in many cases, we obey our families ahead of God.

Family idolatry steals our joy. Perhaps you've heard this saying: "A parent is only as happy as their unhappiest child." I used to quote that. Then I realized how unbiblical it is. Joy is listed as a fruit of the Spirit in Galatians 5:22. In other words, if God lives in you, you should have joy, no matter your circumstances. If even God Himself can't give you joy when one of your children is unhappy, then that means family is your true god. Let's put it more precisely: If you're single, and you think you can't possibly imagine happiness without being married; if you're childless and you think you must have children for life to be complete; if you're married and you think you can never be happy again until your marriage improves; if you have kids and you can't allow yourself to enjoy life if one of your kids is struggling, then those are all signs that family is your true god.

Please understand: I'm not trying to minimize the sorrow one's family situation can cause. It's not wrong to feel sad, to pray for God's help, to weep over them. But if God is your true God, you will also be able to rejoice during times like that. If family is your true god, you'll be filled with despair. You won't want to live. To put it another way, if family is your true god, you're trusting in human beings to provide you with what only God can provide. They will let you down, guaranteed. And when it happens, it will be devastating. What happens when your spouse disappoints you? What happens when your child won't speak to you? What happens when a family member passes away? A family is a wonderful thing, but it's a very fragile god. Worship it, and your heart is guaranteed to be broken sooner or later.

88

The apostle Paul was a single man, which was extremely rare among Jewish men of his time. He was also celibate, which was absolutely unheard of in the Greek cities where he lived. Yet we get no indication Paul was lonely; He was full of joy and freedom. As we saw in chapter 4, he considered his singleness a gift from God. That's hard for us to comprehend; We put such an emphasis on family, we think a person can't possibly be fulfilled without one. By the way, Paul didn't love his singleness because he wanted to be able to throw his dirty underwear on the floor and play video games all day. He knew that God's call on his life was to go to dangerous places to preach the Gospel. If he had been a family man, he would have worried, "What will happen to my wife and kids if I die? Who's going to take care of them?" But as it was, when he was in prison in Rome, he could write to the Philippians and say, "I'm happy if they let me go, or if they cut off my head. If they kill me, I'm with Jesus, and if they release me, I get to keep serving Him. I can't lose!" Listen: If you are single, divorced, or widowed, you are complete, just as you are. And if you're married, no matter how healthy or unhealthy your marriage is, no matter how happy or unhappy your kids are, you can't possibly lose the joy Christ gives you...unless you make your family your true god.

Family idolatry crushes our family. Ephesians 6:4 gives us some great parenting advice. Paul has been writing about how husbands and wives should treat each other. Next, he tells children to obey their parents. Finally, he says to parents (he uses the term "fathers" referring to both moms and dads): *Fathers, do not provoke your children to anger.* That doesn't mean we should never make our kids angry. The Bible has a lot to say about how we as parents are responsible for disciplining our kids. Trust me, if your kids are never angry with you, you're not doing your job. But it doesn't say, "Fathers, keep those kids in line." Some translations put it this way: *do not exasperate your children.* It refers to putting burdens on your kids that they can't possibly bear. Naturally, that rules out overbearing discipline or abuse, but I believe it goes further than that. Many parents exasperate their children by imposing expectations that crush them. Many kids are frustrated and miserable because they feel like they can never be what their parents want them to be. I'm sure none of us ever intends to do that to our kids. But here's one way that happens, in spite of our best intentions: When our kids are born, we have dreams about their future. We picture how wonderful it will be to watch our little girl score the winning goal in the soccer match, or to be chosen prom queen; to see our son quarterback his team to a state title or walk across the stage as valedictorian. We imagine all the fun we'll have with them sharing our favorite pastimes, such as hunting, fishing, golfing, music or watching ball games.

Then our kids come, and they aren't who we thought they would be. Your little princess has no desire to ever wear a dress. Your little cowboy doesn't enjoy riding horses. Whereas you were one of the "cool kids," she may find her place with the outcasts. He may prefer bass guitars to baseballs. She may not be the kind of student you hoped she would be. He may be an introvert instead of the Type-A alpha male you see in yourself. For that matter, many kids struggle with physical, mental or emotional disabilities. Are you able to adjust your expectations, so that you can love the child God gave you, instead of wishing for the child you once dreamed of? If family is your idol, you'll make your kids miserable. You'll tell yourself, "I push them because I love them. It's for their own good." But isn't it also because you want parenting to go the way you dreamed it would?

The alternative to exasperating your kids is *bring them up in the training and instruction of the Lord* (that's the rest of Ephesians 6:4). Your primary job as a parent isn't to steer them toward popularity and success. It's to introduce them to Jesus and show them how to walk with Him. Your child may not share any of your interests, and may not show evidence of any of your strengths...and if so, it will feel disappointing. But if God is your true God, your real focus is to say, "Come with me as I follow Jesus. Let's do this together. Let's talk about the passage you studied in Life Group this Sunday morning. Let's pray for your friend whose dad just lost his job, and maybe take them a gift card from a restaurant. Let's go on this mission trip as a family. Let's help our elderly neighbor with his yard work." Of course, we can't guarantee our kids will choose to follow Christ, any more than we can ensure that they'll get into Harvard or earn a six-figure salary before they're thirty. But you can love the kid they are, instead of the kid you wish you had. You can live out the Christian life before them in such a way that they see how wise and fulfilling it is to follow Jesus. You can pray for their soul even more diligently than you do for their batting average or their GPA. And you can equip yourself to teach them the truths of Scripture even better than you teach them to hit a sand wedge, or tune up an engine. Your kids will be eternally grateful if you do.

The same principle applies to marriage, by the way. So much marital pain would be eliminated if we dealt with our idolatrous expectations. A man falls madly in love with a stunning beauty, thinking, "If she is my wife, I will be the happiest man on earth, as long as I live." But as the years go by, her appearance changes, and so do his feelings for her. The euphoria is gone, replaced by a daily relationship with someone he doesn't even like. A woman marries a man very different from her domineering father, thinking that his carefree personality will be just what she needs to finally make her feel accepted. But she soon realizes that her insecurities are still there, and she now interprets his personality as indifference toward the stability she needs. We all bring expectations into marriage; but when we confess them before God, and understand that only His love can make us complete, we are finally able to love the spouse we have, instead of the impossible one we would create for ourselves if we could. When we worship the Lord, not our fantasy of what marriage "should" be like, He teaches us to love. He makes us, through the process of spiritual growth, into the kind of person our spouse needs us to be.

Do you want to really love your family? Love God with all your heart. Look again at Matthew 10:39: *Whoever finds his life will lose it, and whoever loses his life for my sake will find it.* If you make it your ultimate goal to have a perfect marriage and happy, well-adjusted kids, you will lose your family. Your expectations will crush them. Even if, by sheer force of will, you get them to turn out the way you want, they'll move away from home, or pass away, and you'll be devastated. But if you say, "Lord, the best thing I can do is love you with all my heart," His Spirit will shape you, rubbing off all the hard edges, teaching you to love like He loves, and making you a blessing to your family. You'll be a husband who enjoys putting his wife's needs ahead of his own. You'll be a wife who finds joy in making her husband happy. You'll be a parent who shows your children what the love of God looks like in human flesh. Or you'll be a single adult who shows the world that Jesus is all the joy, peace and purpose you need, whether you get married someday or not. By "dying" to your self-centered expectations of family life, you find the will of God.

I need to be clear: I'm not saying that worshipping God alone is some secret "life hack" that will give you the perfect family you've always wanted. There are no perfect families...even in the Bible. Actually, biblical families experienced profound troubles. Consider:

Abraham and Sarah are among several couples in Scripture who struggled with infertility. In their case, their desperation to conceive a baby led them to a terrible violation of their slave girl, Hagar. The ripple effects of that decision led to conflict between two races for thousands of years.

Jacob, the patriarch (and namesake) of the nation of Israel, had children born to four different mothers, all of whom lived in the same household. Not surprisingly, it wasn't a happy home, to put it mildly: The sons in the family sold one of their brothers, Joseph, into slavery, then lied to their father, telling him the boy was killed by an animal.

Jacob himself grew up in a dysfunctional family. He was his mother's favorite, while his twin brother Esau was favored by their father. The resulting sibling rivalry tore the family apart.

King David was a man after God's own heart. But his family was a trainwreck...and it was at least partially his fault. The record includes adultery, deception, incestuous rape, murder, and one of David's own sons forcing him violently from the throne.

Biblical heroes like Aaron, Samuel and Gideon had to watch as their own children turned against their teachings and the Lord.

And yes, that includes the family of Jesus. When He first began His ministry, His brothers didn't believe in Him. They made fun of Him. Later, Mary and her sons came to take Jesus home by force, because they thought He had lost His mind. We can imagine why they felt this way. Jesus, as the oldest son, was expected by society to take care of his mother, who was probably widowed (Joseph is never mentioned after Jesus is twelve). Yet Jesus was a homeless wandering would-be Messiah, not providing for the family, so they likely resented having to bear the financial burden that He was unable to fulfill. Besides that, they heard the kinds of things the religious leaders were saying about Him. In a small town like Nazareth, I'm sure they were the subject of plenty of gossip. Besides, would you like to be the little brother of Jesus? Do you think they ever got tired of hearing "Why can't you be more like Jesus?"

I recount these stories not to depress you, but to prove that there is literally no way to have a problem-free family. Families are made up of sinners living in a sin-stained world, and so there will be trouble at times. Love your family. Serve them in the name of Jesus. Enjoy the countless blessings you share with them through the years. But don't build your identity and hopes on them. Don't expect them to meet your every need for love and acceptance. Only God can do that.

Let's return to the example of Jesus and His family. It's clear that, even though they caused Him pain at times, Jesus loved His family. One of the last things He did before dying on the cross was ask His disciple John to take care of His mother. But He did not idolize them.

What if He had? Imagine Jesus had said, "My family comes first." He wouldn't have left home to preach and work miracles. He would have stayed in Nazareth, working as a carpenter and taking care of His mother. He would have gotten discouraged when He found out His own brothers didn't believe in Him. He would have said, "If I can't even convince my own flesh and blood, there's no use trying to take the Good News to the whole world." And He never would have gone to Jerusalem, where the religious leaders were waiting to arrest and kill Him. Think of it: If Jesus had idolized His family, He would never have died in our place. We would still be lost. Because Jesus didn't idolize His family, He saved us...and saved them too.

Chapter 8

When Faith Goes Bad: The Idol of Religion

Perhaps you've heard the saying, "Christianity isn't a religion; it's a relationship." That's not actually true. Christianity has certain doctrines we must believe, or we're not actually serving the God of Scripture. We have certain commands we choose to follow, and rituals we perform to serve God. If you have doctrines, rules, and rituals, you have a religion. What we should say is "Christianity isn't just a religion; it's a relationship," because those beliefs, rules and practices are worth nothing without that personal relationship with God through Jesus Christ. But what if our religion gets in the way of our relationship with Him? Is that even possible? Could we believe all the right things, do all the right stuff, avoid all the big sins, and still miss God? I believe so. I believe that religion itself can be an idol that keeps us from devoting ourselves fully to Christ. I believe we can be morally upright and doctrinally correct, and experience none of the joy that comes from following Christ, and worse still, can drive people away from salvation. I believe this because Jesus clearly believed it. In His teaching ministry, He constantly drew a clear line between those whose love for God had transformed them, and those who used religious devotion as a tool for their own selfish benefit.

In Matthew 23, Jesus stands in Jerusalem, the political and spiritual capital of His people, and preaches a scathing message against two specific groups within Judaism, the scribes and the Pharisees. Scholars and preachers often refer to this chapter as the "Seven Woes" because seven times, Jesus says, "woe to you, scribes and Pharisees." The people who first heard this message must have found Jesus' choice of targets astonishing. The scribes were the religious professionals of Israel. It was their job to interpret the Word of God and make sure the people were following it. The Pharisees, on the other hand, weren't clergy; they were highly devout laymen who had committed themselves to keeping Israel on track spiritually. They were descended from the Hasidim, a group of fiercely patriotic men who had won a revolution, defeating the godless pagans who ruled Israel and defiled their temple, and ushering in nearly a hundred years of independence (Jews celebrate this event at Hanukah). It's a fair bet if you and I had lived in Israel 2000 years ago, we would have admired the scribes and Pharisees; they were seen as heroes.

So why did Jesus criticize them? There were plenty of other groups in Israel at the time who seemed more deserving of His scorn. The Herodians were committed to supporting the descendants of Herod the Great, one of the worst leaders of all time, whose offspring were equally corrupt and immoral. Yet Jesus never says a word against them in the Gospels. The Zealots preached bloody violence against Israel's enemies. I am sure Jesus' teachings about loving our enemies and turning the other cheek irritated them, but He never condemned the Zealots as a group; in fact, He made one of them a member of the Twelve. For that matter, what about the Romans themselves? Their culture was full of pagan worship, sexual immorality, greed, and violence; and they constantly showed disrespect for Israel and its God. But He didn't condemn them either.

In the ultimate irony, the scribes and Pharisees were committed to keeping Israel from idolatry. That was their mission. Throughout Israel's history, the people had been spiritually fickle, chasing after the gods of other nations. Eventually, that led to their nation's destruction, and seventy years of captivity. The scribes and Pharisees said, "Never again." They would keep God's people faithful to the covenant of Moses, or die trying. Yet in their zeal to keep the people from idolatry, they fell into an idolatry of their own. Throughout His earthly ministry, Jesus publicly jousted with these two revered groups. Finally, in the days just before His impending crucifixion, Jesus laid it all on the line in a withering indictment of false religion.

Jesus begins by saying, *The scribes and the Pharisees sit on Moses' seat, so do and observe whatever they tell you, but not the works they do. For they preach, but do not practice.* (vv. 2-3) One way of paraphrasing what Jesus says here is, "Don't be like them. They have the religion, but not the relationship." He ends the sermon with these poignant words: *O Jerusalem, Jerusalem, the city that kills the prophets and stones those who are sent to it! How often would I have gathered your children together as a hen gathers her brood under her wings, and you were not willing! See, your house is left to you desolate. For I tell you, you will not see me again, until you say, 'Blessed is he who comes in the name of the Lord* (vv. 37-39). Within the lifetime of most of those hearing His words, the city will be destroyed, most of its walls knocked to the ground, and the temple demolished. It has never been rebuilt. God's people believed all the right doctrines, followed the right rules, and practiced the right rituals, and it wasn't enough. They put their faith in their religion, but didn't know God, and it cost them everything.

I'm going to say a terrible thing. We often talk about the decline of Christianity in our culture. While the Gospel is spreading like wildfire in places like China, Africa and South America, it seems stalled here. We like to blame lots of different groups: The media, atheists, other religious groups, millennials (we love to blame them for everything). But I think the primary blame lies with us. Sadly, as I read Matthew 23 today, I can't help thinking that the religion that calls itself by Christ's own name often has more in common with His enemies than with Him. You and I can't change American evangelicalism on our own. Only God can do that; that's why we pray for revival. But we can search our own hearts. Revival could begin right here with us. So here's a series of questions, based on Matthew 23, to determine if your religion has taken the place of your relationship to God.

Do I practice "religious image management"? Six times in this sermon, Jesus called the scribes and Pharisees "hypocrites." Prior to Jesus, that was the Greek term for an actor. Actors in those days wore oversized masks to show the emotion they were trying to convey. And that is the point Jesus was trying to get across: These scribes and Pharisees were wearing a mask, playing a part. They actually were exceptionally good at keeping the Law; but they did it to impress people. In v. 5 He says, *They do all their deeds to be seen by others.* He gave several examples. For instance, in Jewish life at that time, men wore certain garments to remind themselves of their duty to serve God. One was a phylactery, or a small leather box they wore on their wrist or forehead. Inside the box was contained a copy of Deuteronomy 6:4, *Hear O Israel, the Lord our God, the Lord is one.* In Deuteronomy 6:8, God commanded the Jews to bind this command on their hands and foreheads, and they took Him literally. Another garment was the tassel, or the fringe on the edges of their outer robes. In Numbers, the Jews were told to put tassels on the edges of their robes to remind themselves of God's commandments. Jesus did this; remember the woman who touched the fringes of His garment and was healed? But the religious leaders had turned this into a sort of competition. They wore wide phylacteries and long tassels so people would think they were more righteous than others. In other words, they were actors playing a part.

We still do this. We use our carefully curated photos on social media to let everyone know how well we're doing (#blessed!). We gather on Sundays, wearing our best, and let no one know what we're struggling with. Oh, we might share prayer requests in our small groups, but never anything that reveals our true failings, such as "My anger is tearing a hole in our marriage that may never heal." "I'm so resentful toward my boss that I'm making myself and everyone around me miserable. I need to learn to love Him like Jesus loves me, in spite of my sin." "I'm an addict. I have been for years and always will be. But I know God can deliver me. I need your prayers." Jesus created the Church to make disciples, and that requires openness, true community. So when one believer chooses to be transparent and vulnerable, it can become contagious. When you have the courage to share what you're really struggling with, others will find that courage inside themselves, too.

Am I better at keeping score of others or drawing others to the Lord? Here's v. 4: *They tie up heavy burdens, hard to bear, and lay them on people's shoulders, but they themselves are not willing to move them with their finger...*and v. 13: *For you shut the kingdom of heaven in people's faces. For you neither enter yourselves nor allow those who would enter to go in.* One of the things the scribes and Pharisees hated most about Jesus was that He was "a friend of sinners." To them, there were certain sins that rendered a person untouchable. Sexual sin and collecting taxes for the Romans were considered especially terrible; people who did those things weren't welcome in the synagogue. Yet those were precisely the people who couldn't get enough of Jesus. We all have our ways of evaluating others. For example, when I was growing up, if I heard someone using profane language, I immediately assumed they couldn't possibly be a Christian. As I grew up in the faith, I realized that while God certainly does care about the language we use, that trait alone is not a surefire indicator of righteousness. Some of the meanest, most vindictive people I've ever known have never used a four-letter word in their lives. I heard another preacher say that in the church where he grew up, a person who smoked cigarettes would never have been accepted as a spiritual leader. Certainly, one can make a biblical case that since smoking harms the body—which belongs to God— Christians should abstain. But in that same church, people could be deacons or Sunday school teachers despite being quick-tempered, unforgiving, racist, or greedy, and no one batted an eye. For that matter, no one ever preached against gluttony, even though that sin is surely as harmful to the body as smoking.

That's what idolatrous religion does to us. It makes us good at keeping score of others, by helping us form a list of "boundary markers" that determine who's in and who's out. But that's not the calling of Jesus. Nowhere in the teachings of Christ or His apostles are we given a set of criteria by which to decide if someone else is a good person or not. Instead, we're commanded to love our neighbor, to seek first the Kingdom of God, to make disciples of all nations. In other words, our job is not to decide who's in and who's out; it's to draw people to the Savior. So, how are you doing? How many people are you intentionally trying to influence toward Christ? If you say, "I don't know any lost people personally," then go out and meet some. Walk across the cul-de-sac to get to know your neighbors. Join a gym. Talk to the other parents at your kids' baseball game. Volunteer for prison ministry or at the hospital. Most of all, pray for unbelievers by name, and for opportunities ("divine appointments") to make Christ known to them. The Gospel accounts show that the most scandalous sinners were the people who were most attracted to Jesus. Today, those kinds of people wouldn't consider going to a church. What changed? Jesus didn't. He's still exactly what lost people are hungry for. We're the ones who've changed...for the worse. They don't come to our churches because they don't see Jesus in us. Let's do something about that.

Do I put religious leaders on a pedestal? Here's a little "trade secret" among pastors: It's conventional wisdom that one shouldn't become pastor of a church after a long-term, beloved leader retires or dies. No matter how healthy and promising the church, your tenure there will be brief and painful. A large segment of the congregation will never accept you. You can't possibly measure up to the man who fed and shepherded them so faithfully all those years. Many will leave the church, while others will stay, but will constantly criticize you. As I say, that's conventional wisdom, and there are exceptions. But I have seen it happen often enough to make the conventional wisdom seem like established fact. That should make us all deeply sad. After all, who are we worshipping at church? Is it the pastor, or Jesus? If Jesus is the one being exalted at our church, shouldn't we be able to worship there no matter what we think of the guy who stands behind the pulpit for thirty minutes a week? Of course, pastors are not above criticism—more on that in a moment. And yes, there are biblically defensible reasons to leave a church. But if our basis for leaving is that, "My pastor's sermons don't feed me," or "I really like the way that Rev. So-and-So preaches," or "I just miss Brother Bob," then perhaps we're actually worshipping a religious leader instead of the One who saved us.

To make matters worse, the last hundred years have seen the rise of the Celebrity Preacher. An entire cottage industry has been built around marketing the sermons and books of particularly "anointed" men of God. Most Christians have their favorites, and we endow them with amazing authority over our lives. Then, when they fall—as they all too often do—the trauma is devastating. In 2021, a podcast by Christianity Today Media, The Rise and Fall of Mars Hill, told the story of one such preacher, Mark Driscoll. An insanely talented, dynamic leader, Driscoll helped start a church in the unlikeliest of places—Seattle. It grew quickly, and just as rapidly, Driscoll's star rose in the evangelical community. He wrote bestselling books, spoke to auditoriums full of pastors at leadership conferences, and pastored a mega-church—all before he turned thirty. And just as quickly, it all fell apart. The Rise and Fall of Mars Hill shows the tragedy of treating a successful preacher like more than a man. We give such a leader power because he's gifted, without asking if he possesses the maturity to wield it. We allow him to surround himself with yes-men, and refrain from confronting obvious flaws, because we don't want to hinder something so effective. We put a man on a pedestal, and it does immense harm to the cause of Christ.

In verses 6-12, Jesus says of the scribes and Pharisees, *...and they love the place of honor at feasts and the best seats in the synagogues and greetings in the marketplaces and being called rabbi by others. But you are not to be called rabbi, for you have one teacher, and you are all brothers. And call no man your father on earth, for you have one Father, who is in heaven. Neither be called instructors, for you have one instructor, the Christ. The greatest among you shall be your servant. Whoever exalts himself will be humbled, and whoever humbles himself will be exalted.*

Jesus knows that there is an inner narcissist in all of us. When a leader—even a gifted Christian leader—is treated like an untouchable hero, that inner narcissist takes control. In these verses, He's not just talking about forsaking titles and perks. He's telling us to treat our leaders like fellow sinners. True, the New Testament tells us to show honor to those who lead us spiritually. Hebrews 13:17, for instance, reminds us that these are the people who watch over our souls. It's a hard job, and we should do all we can to make it a joy for them, not a ball and chain. Encourage those who lead your church. Pray for them. Go out of your way to bless their families. Ministerial burnout is a serious problem; advocate for your church staff, that they will have the financial support and the time off they need. But when you see behavior in them that concerns you, speak to them about it. Don't be afraid to confront sin or sloppy teaching, biblically and graciously but firmly. And as for The Celebrity Preacher, maintain an emotional distance. If there's a well-known leader whose work you find particularly helpful, that's fine. But listen to other voices as well. And make sure your primary source of external spiritual sustenance is at the local church level, where you can observe the lifestyles of your leaders and judge them by the fruits of their character, not just by the flashiness of their products.

Do I think because I'm good at being religious, God will bless me? In v. 23, Jesus says, *you tithe mint and dill and cumin, and have neglected the weightier matters of the law: justice and mercy and faithfulness. These* *you ought to have done, without neglecting the others.* All observant Jews practiced tithing: They gave 10% of everything they made to God. But the scribes and Pharisees went even further. They gave 10% of the herbs in their flowerbeds. That amounted to pennies. But to them, it was a way of proving to everyone, including themselves, that they were better than regular folks. Some of us would have to say we're pretty good at the religion thing. I'd bet most of us are. Churches may not be attracting lost people the way Jesus did, but we're still attracting people who are good at religion; people who find it fairly easy to be outwardly moral and to follow the rules.

We are all familiar with the parable of the Prodigal Son. What most people don't know is that the main character in the story wasn't the son who ran away from home; it was the older brother who stayed behind. Put this book down for a moment and read Luke 15. Notice that the climax of the story comes when the Father confronts the older brother. Everything else is a prelude to that moment. He begs the obstinate son to come in and join the celebration for his long-lost sibling. But the older son refuses. His answer amounts to: "Why should I? I've done nothing but play by your rules for years, and it's never paid off for me. This idiot goes out and disgraces our family name, and when he comes home, you throw the party of the year for him!" At the beginning of the chapter (vv. 1-3), did you notice that Jesus was telling this story to the scribes and Pharisees? The older brother represents them. They were good at being moral and religious, but that didn't mean they loved their Heavenly Father any more than the prostitutes and tax collectors they hated. They served Him so that they could get something out of Him, and that's not love. This applies today to all us rule-keeping religious types: Do you think God owes you a certain standard of living for all your good deeds? When something you prayed for doesn't happen, do you get resentful and wonder, "When is all this righteousness going to pay off?" If so, that's religious idolatry talking.

When did I last repent? All through history, the people sent by God to tell us the truth have been unpopular, even hated. Jesus talks about this in Matthew 23:35, mentioning two such people. The first one is Abel, part of the first family in human history, killed by his brother because Cain was jealous of Abel's righteousness. The second is Zechariah, a man who was stoned to death at the command of the king of Israel, because he dared to call out Israel's idolatry. Abel's story is found in the first few chapters of the Bible, in Genesis. Zechariah's story is recorded toward the end of 2 Chronicles, which was the last book of the Hebrew Bible in Jesus' day. So essentially, Jesus is saying, "From the beginning of God's Word to the end, from A to Z, you have rejected everything I have tried to tell you." The Pharisees knew all these stories. They wanted to prove they were different from their rebellious forefathers. And so they would build monuments over the tombs of the prophets. It was their way of saying, "If the prophets had been alive today, we would not have killed them. We would have responded to the Word of God." But Jesus said, "You are no different than your forefathers. They killed the prophets, and you will kill my apostles, who I send out in my name to give you the good news." For all their outward righteousness, the scribes and Pharisees were too proud to admit they were still sinners in need of God's grace. They never repented. And without repentance, there is no righteousness, no relationship with the God who saves.

Let's be clear about this: God is not impressed by your religious resume. That's not what He's looking for. When did you last repent? Repentance means more than, "I admit I'm not perfect," more than, "Lord, forgive us for the many ways we've failed you," more even than, "I sure wish I hadn't done that." Repentance is a deep-seated, sorrowful desire that says "God, I never want to go down that road again, and I will do whatever you say, sacrifice anything you require, if it will lead to change and renewal. Right now, I just need your grace, because doing it on my own is obviously a recipe for disaster." Religious folks tend to think of repentance as something we do at the beginning of our faith journey; it's how one becomes a Christian. But Scripture says without consistent repentance, we can't really follow Christ.

So what happens whenever your sin gets confronted? Do you get angry and defensive? Perhaps you make excuses, rationalize, or blame other people: "I know it's wrong, but it's the way I was raised," or "It's no big deal. I'm still better than most people." Do you quickly change the subject? When you stop repenting, you stop growing. And when you stop growing toward God, you step out of relationship with

Him. You're like a teenager telling his parent, "I'll follow your rules, but I don't need for us to get any closer." If you can't remember the last time you changed the way you think, or attacked a bad habit, or genuinely apologized to someone you hurt, or got down on your knees and said, "Lord, please change me," ask God what needs to be repented of. In fact, now would be a good time to ask Him that question, no matter what.

Just remember how that prodigal son tale ends. The end of the story is the father pleading with the older brother, "Come on in and celebrate." Jesus left His most famous story with a cliffhanger; we don't know what that older brother ultimately chose to do. That's because Jesus was using that story to plead with those scribes and Pharisees. For all the hatred they poured on Him, for all their pride and hypocrisy and religious idolatry, He loved those men. He loved them enough to die for them, and He soon would do just that. He was pleading, "Don't just stay out here following rules. Come into my Father's house and celebrate His grace. I want you to share in that life with me." He makes that same plea to you and me today. I'm not trying to get any child of God to doubt her salvation. I'm just saying it's likely that most churches contain people who know how to play the part, but don't really know Him. Could that be true of you? And there are also people who would say, "I remember when I was close to my Father, excited about being in His presence, and growing day by day…but that's been a long time ago." Nothing is more important than your relationship with Him. He died to make it possible. Now He waits for you to join the party. Let go of your religious idolatry and throw yourself into the arms of a Father who loves you.

Chapter 9

Between Washington and Jerusalem: The Idol of Politics

In the Fall of 2016, a friend invited me to a lunch hosted by a ministry he was part of. The guest speaker that day was a well-known Christian athlete, but before he spoke, the leader of the ministry took the microphone to welcome us. His first words were, "I'd like to say hello to all my fellow deplorables." There were a few chuckles in the room. We all knew he was referring to Hilary Clinton's infamous recent comment, in which she called Donald Trump voters "a basket of deplorables." He stood there for a moment, grim-faced, shaking his head, letting those words settle over the crowd. Then, he introduced our guest speaker, and his words were seemingly forgotten. But here's what I found interesting: Not only did none of us seem surprised that he would make such a partisan political comment at a gathering of Christians, but no one seemed concerned that his words might keep someone from coming to Christ. The event was held at lunch during a workday, in hopes that members of the organization would invite their co-workers, particularly non-Christians, to attend and hear the Gospel. What if some of those non-Christians in attendance were politically liberal? I felt certain that the chairman would never think of greeting such a crowd with words like "Hello to all my fellow white guys." After all, he wouldn't want a non-white person to think that only people of his race were welcome to follow Jesus. So why didn't he have the same concern about unbelievers on the other side of the political aisle?

At the start of this book, I compared idolatry to cancer. I stand by that analogy. Idolatry in all its forms is deadly to our spiritual lives, and must be rooted out. But in my role as a pastor, I have come to see political idolatry as the most virulent and widespread form of the disease among our nation's Christians today. That's why I have dedicated two chapters, nearly a third of the total pages of this book to this one topic. I believe, in fact, that our political idolatry, more than any other single factor, is what is slowly killing the American Church. We won't see revival occur in our nation until we repent of it. My experience at that lunch event was just one piece of evidence. No one in a room full of devout Christians was the least bit surprised that their organization's chairman had chosen to score some political points in a way that might have kept roughly half of all Americans from considering Christ. I have quite a bit more evidence, and I'll get to that soon enough. But first, notice that I saved this subject for the last chapter. That was strategic. I know that what I write here will make some of you angry, and I wanted to be sure you read the other chapters before you threw this book in the garbage, lit it aflame on your barbecue grill, or blasted it to smithereens with your 12 gauge. But before you do any of those things, please read the following two disclaimers:

First, I'm not saying that Christians should stay out of politics. Here in America, we are blessed with a rare privilege: The right to engage in our nation's self-governance. That's an opportunity we cannot pass up. To shun the political process because it's messy and sometimes ugly would be like refusing to help poor people because they make us feel uncomfortable. Part of the process of spiritual growth is attaining wisdom, or the ability to make moral choices through seeing as God sees. As we grow in that wisdom, we should let it guide us in our voting decisions. Some Christians, in fact, should consider running for office. If God has given us wisdom and truth, shouldn't we bring those into the public square? Shouldn't we love our neighbors enough to help them build a better country?

Second, I'm not saying that being politically moderate is inherently more righteous than being partisan. In this chapter, I'm going to take some shots at both sides of the political aisle (although, since my tribe is primarily conservative, I will spend more time exposing our blind spots than those who disagree with us). You might, therefore, think that I am arguing that all Christians should be political centrists. So let me say this clearly: If you believe one political party is clearly better than the other, by all means work to advance that party's agenda. Just don't give your political beliefs and activities the place in your life that only God deserves.

What does political idolatry look like? And why do I believe the American church is infected with it? Here are three signs I see:

Rampant fear. Around 700 years before Christ, a young man named Ahaz became King of Judah. Almost immediately, he was confronted by a foreign policy crisis. The nations of Israel and Syria had formed a coalition to oppose the expansion of the Assyrian empire. The Assyrians were numerous, warlike and ruthless. Delegates from Israel[viii] and Syria both demanded that King Ahaz send his Judean army to help fight against them. When Ahaz hesitated, the coalition threatened to invade Judah and replace him with a King who would do what they said. In those days, Isaiah the prophet advised the Kings of Judah, and he urged this young King not to be afraid. He promised that these two nations would be devastated long before they could muster up the armies to invade his land. He gave Ahaz a sign: *Behold, the virgin shall conceive and bear a son, and shall call his name Immanuel…For before the boy knows how to refuse the evil and choose the good, the land whose two kings you dread will be deserted* (Isaiah 7:14 and 16)[ix].

Isaiah urged the King to trust God rather than political alliances to save the nation: *If you do not stand firm in your faith, you will not stand at all* (Isaiah 7:9, NIV). But Ahaz refused to listen. Instead, he allied himself with the King of Assyria, which is like inviting a mountain lion into your house to deal with a mouse problem. Assyria invaded Israel, devastating that land and erasing ten of the twelve Jewish tribes. And Ahaz's son would later face an invasion of Judah by that same empire. They left Ahaz alone, but only because he paid heavy tributes to them. Later, Ahaz went to Assyria to visit the King who had "saved" him. He saw the altar that the Assyrians used to worship their gods, and ordered one just like it to be placed in the temple in Jerusalem. He adopted the awful practices of foreign Kings, including burning his own son in a fiery offering to the pagan god Molech.

It was only one of many times Israel was led astray by a King who trusted political power more than the power of God. It shouldn't surprise us; God's original plan was that His people would have no King but Himself. He promised to protect and provide for them so abundantly, other nations would be drawn to their light. But the people begged the prophet Samuel to give them a King. When the prophet warned them that a King would tax them, would draft their children into his service and impoverish them, they answered back, *No! But there shall be a King over us, that we also may be like all the nations, and that our king may judge us and go out before us and fight our battles* (1 Samuel 8:19)." Do you hear what they're saying? "We are afraid. We want someone to fight our battles for us. We don't trust the Lord to do it, so we want to gain power and security the way everyone else does." They trusted political leaders to do for them what only God can do. They ignored the promises of God and the history of His miraculous intervention on their behalf. They were afraid, and in times of rampant fear, someone we can see, hear and touch seems more trustworthy than an invisible God. They trusted in human rulers, and those rulers ultimately led them away from God. In the end, the very thing they feared the most—invasion and destruction of their nation—happened anyway.

Today, political discourse in our country is infused with the language of fear. Here's one example: As you might expect, religious freedom is the political issue that matters the most to me personally. Whatever else a politician might stand for, if they don't have a commitment to freedom of worship, I will not vote for them. I subscribe to the newsletters of various organizations that defend religious liberty. Although I believe in the work these organizations do, I am consistently disappointed in the tone of their rhetoric.

American Christians possess a freedom of religion unique in the history of the world, and while there are certainly people in our culture who would love to take that away, our freedom to worship as we choose has never been more secure than it is today. But the emails these groups send out make it sound as though we're only days away from government thugs invading our church and dragging the entire ministry staff to jail without trial. I know that's true of organizations of all kinds, including both political parties; the surest way to motivate donors and mobilize voters is by stoking fear. No matter what issue we care about the most, the message is the same: "You are in terrible danger. We are your only hope. Support us, or you have only yourselves to blame for the coming destruction of America."

As Christians, we should be the ones who refuse to fall for the rhetoric of fear, who say along with the Psalmist, *Some trust in chariots and some in horses, but we trust in the name of the Lord our God* (Psalm 20:7). Unfortunately, that's not what I see happening among believers today. When I hear Christians talk about current events, there's a sense of desperation in their voices. Every election is "the most important election of our lives." I remember talking to a Christian friend the day after a presidential election in which the "other guy" won. She was distraught. She even felt angry with God for allowing this to happen. I tried to tell her that since we vote on our leaders, perhaps we have only ourselves to blame for the outcome. And if God does decide the winner of elections, then surely this man was God's man for our nation at this time, even if he wasn't the one either of us had voted for. But she refused to believe this. In her mind, God had failed us, and she couldn't understand why.

Demonization of the other side. In her 2020 book *Strange Rites: New Religions for a Godless World,* Tara Isabella Burton identifies Social Justice Culture as one of the three fastest-growing religions in America today. I doubt that anyone would identify "Social Justice" as their religion, but Burton (who, by the way, is neither an Evangelical nor a conservative) writes that many Americans are finding in their political advocacy the things people have historically found in traditional religion. For example, there's conversion to a life dedicated to something larger than self (which was known as becoming "woke" until conservatives began using that term as an insult). There's ritual (marches and other activism), doctrine ("Trans women ARE women," "American prosperity was built on systemic racism"), and, of course, there are enemies. These include racism, sexism, homophobia, and any number of problems that virtually all decent people of any party oppose. But followers of Social Justice Culture believe they alone have the authority to define those terms, and identify who falls on the side of evil. This is why a writer who is overwhelmingly kind and just in all her dealings can be "outed" as a racist because (in the minds of self-appointed judges) too few of the characters in her stories are non-white. Or a business leader who has consistently fair hiring practices is nevertheless labeled a bigot because he attends a church that teaches a biblical view of marriage. This new religion even has its own form of excommunication: being "cancelled." That's the dark side of religion: It gives us a justification to feel superior toward outsiders. In our self-righteousness, we think opposing them is the way of holiness. At its worst, this instinct leads us to see our enemies as something less than human, not worthy of the same rights and privileges as us.

Does Christianity have that same dark side? Occasionally, I see Christians post links to sermons on social media, saying, "Listen to this. I wish all preachers could be this brave." Every time, it's a sermon about the evils of liberalism, or why we should reject the latest Democratic presidential candidate. Recently, a church in my area promoted an upcoming sermon series that would expose the Satanic agenda behind Critical Race Theory, Socialism, and "wokeness." The comments from Facebook users praised the church for being so courageous in tackling these subjects. As someone who preaches every week, trust me on this: It takes absolutely zero courage to preach a message that almost all of your congregation agrees with. Courageous, biblical preaching exposes OUR hidden sins, not the flaws of people outside the church. It challenges us to win outsiders to Christ, not condemn them as threats to our way of life.

There were political factions in the time of Jesus, as well. One group favored the Herods. It would have been quite natural for Jesus to speak out against anyone who supported the corrupt family that had tried to kill Him when He was an infant (see Matthew 2). He didn't do that. But Luke 8:3 says that Joanna, the wife of Herod's household manager, became one of His closest followers, and helped finance His ministry. Another group, the Zealots, preached violence against Israel's enemies. Jesus clearly didn't agree with this philosophy, but He included one of them among His Twelve disciples (Luke 6:15). Simon the Zealot overcame his extremist political views because of the Gospel. And then there were the Romans. Jesus could have scored easy political points by condemning the elite Jews who collaborated with the Empire that oppressed His people. He could have railed against the Romans themselves for their pagan religion, their violence and injustice, and their horrible sexual ethics. There is no record in the Gospels of Jesus doing this. Instead, He used a Roman centurion's faith as an example to His Jewish followers, and started a movement that converted hundreds of thousands of Romans in the centuries to come.

So a preacher who uses his pulpit to demonize people he disagrees with is anything but courageous, and he's certainly not Christlike. And when we as Christians revel in our hatred and mockery of politicians who we oppose, we're giving in to the dark side of religion. In fact, the religion we're following in that moment is not the way of Jesus. It's allegiance to the idol of political power. Ironically, we're bowing before the same false god as the people we hate.

Willingness to compromise biblical behavior in order to achieve political goals. For many years, politically active Christians were known as "Values Voters." Politicians knew they needed to uphold certain moral standards if they wanted our vote. Then came the 2016 election. Looking back, it's almost funny how astonished the media was that Evangelicals overwhelmingly voted for Donald Trump. To me, that wasn't the real surprise. After all, in our political system, we only really have two options, and one of the parties has essentially stopped trying to appeal to people like us. For me, the real surprise was what came in the next four years. I remember lots of conversations among my fellow Christians in the days leading up to November 2016, as they said things like, "I don't like Trump's character or the way he talks, but I can't vote for Clinton." Others promised, "We'll hold him accountable. He'll owe us, and we'll make sure he acts honorably." What happened instead was that, over the next four years, Evangelicals by and large fell in love with Donald Trump, to an extent I've never seen with any President in my lifetime. Not only did we not hold him accountable when he said or did things that—coming from any past President--would have raised massive howls of Christian protest, we became his most strident defenders.

Here's just one example: When President Bill Clinton's "improper relationship" with an intern came to light in 1998, Franklin Graham wrote in *The Wall Street Journal*:

"Last week Mr. Clinton told 70 million Americans that his adulterous actions with Ms. Lewinsky were a "private" matter "between me, the two people I love the most–my wife and our daughter–and our God." But the God of the Bible says that what one does in private does matter...If he will lie to or mislead his wife and daughter, those with whom he is most intimate, what will prevent him from doing the same to the American public?"

Graham went on to write that,

"Mr. Clinton's sin can be forgiven, but he must start by admitting to it and refraining from legalistic doublespeak. According to the Scripture, the president did not have an "inappropriate relationship" with Monica Lewinsky–he committed adultery. He didn't "mislead" his wife and us–he lied. Acknowledgment must be coupled with genuine remorse. A repentant spirit that says, "I'm sorry. I was wrong. I won't do it again.

I ask for your forgiveness," would go a long way toward personal and national healing."[x]

I agreed with every word of that article. Graham was doing the work of a prophet; it was mindful of John the Baptist calling out the disgusting behavior of Herod Antipas (Mark 6).

Twenty years later, the same newspaper (The Wall Street Journal) reported that President Trump had paid $130,000 to an adult film star before the 2016 election to cover up his affair with her. Naturally, reporters asked Graham if the same standards applied. At first, he made a distinction between the two adulteries: Clinton's affair happened while he was in office, while Trump's occurred beforehand. Later, he made the following astonishing argument to the Associated Press: "...there's such bigger problems in front of us as a nation that we need to be dealing with than other things in his life a long time ago. I think some of these things -- that's for him and his wife to deal with."[xi] There was no call for public repentance, no appeal to biblical standards of morality. Instead, the excuse that he rejected two decades before—"this is just between me and my wife"—he now endorsed.

I have great respect for Franklin Graham, especially his Samaritan's Purse ministry, which enables American Christians to share God's love with children around the world. For me, that's one of the frustrating things about the way political idolatry has infiltrated American Evangelicalism; good, Christ-loving people can become so invested in the success of a party, an ideology, or even a specific politician that they don't see how badly they are compromising their witness to the world. The terrible irony is that something similar happened to Franklin's father Billy, who was perhaps the most influential Christian of the Twentieth Century, and a hero of mine. Billy Graham had personal relationships with every President from Harry Truman to George W Bush. Although he certainly had strong political opinions of his own, he didn't let that stop him from ministering to men of widely divergent philosophies in the most pressure-filled job in the world. But with one president, he got too close. Graham and Richard Nixon developed a deep friendship, and Graham spent a great deal of time in the Oval Office. I have no way of knowing how sincere President Nixon was in his feelings for Graham, but members of the Nixon administration undoubtedly used the great evangelist's presence to give themselves a veneer of righteousness, even as they were doing "dirty tricks" behind the scenes. Graham even got caught up in a shameful conversation about American Jews among members of the President's cabinet. When recordings of that conversation were leaked (decades later), Graham admitted he had been too eager to fit in, and said things he wished he could erase. It was a moment that reminded us that even the greatest evangelist of our time was as human as the rest of us. But it also showed us the danger of allowing political loyalties to overshadow our desire to represent Christ well.

Of course, Franklin Graham was far from alone in this. In fact, whenever a prominent Christian did criticize the President, they were roundly attacked. When *Christianity Today* published an editorial calling for Trump to be removed from office, Editor Mark Galli noted that they had made the same call for President Clinton twenty years earlier. Their stance hadn't changed: When it comes to our nation's leader, character matters.[xii] However, this time, the stalwart Evangelical magazine lost many subscribers who had earlier praised them for calling Clinton out. Prominent Christian voices accused them of "turning liberal," even though their doctrinal stance hadn't changed. It didn't matter that the magazine still promoted biblical Christianity; what mattered was that they had cast dirt on the wrong man, in the eyes of some. It quickly became apparent that any well-known Christian who wanted to advance his or her career needed to avoid any hint of disloyalty to the President.

As I wrestled with this dilemma, I found that many Christians I knew were having the same struggle: Why are we treating this President so differently? Why aren't we calling him out the way we have other presidents when they behaved badly? The answer I got as we talked it through tended to sound something like this, "These are desperate times. We're under attack, and we need someone who will be just as tough as our opponents." Family Research Council president Tony Perkins summed up this sentiment in an interview with Politico: "(Evangelicals) were tired of being kicked around by Barack Obama and his leftists. And I think they are finally glad that there's somebody on the playground that is willing to punch the bully." When the reporter asked Perkins what happened to "turn the other cheek," he replied, "You know, you only have two cheeks."[xiii] That sounds disturbingly like the logic King Ahaz used three thousand years ago: "Sure, God has told us that standing firm in Him is the only way to stand. But right now, we need someone flesh-and-blood to fight our battles. We can't be choosy about our savior; if we have to compromise our beliefs in order to please him, so be it. Too much is at stake."

Again, I am not criticizing anyone's vote or support for President Trump. Like all Presidents, I believe he had his strengths and weaknesses, and history will show over the long haul whether he was good or bad for our country. What I find troubling is the sense of unquestioning loyalty that many have shown, and continue to show, toward a mere man, often at the cost of our Christian witness. Non-Christians see our hypocrisy, and it damages our ability to share the Gospel with them.

Making a Difference Without Worshipping Politics

Alright, enough about all the ways we're doing it wrong. Let's talk about the ways we can get it right. I do believe it's possible to faithfully serve Christ as Lord in the political process. But it will take some significant changes, including new habits, new ways of thinking, and new ways of communicating. Here are the steps I see that are necessary for us to reclaim our righteous voice in the public square:

Act like Christians. This one is so obvious, I'll keep it short. Scripture is clear that there are certain markers that should set the people of God apart. In Galatians 5:22-23, we see a list of "fruit" (characteristics) that the Holy Spirit produces: Love, joy, peace, patience, kindness, goodness, faithfulness, gentleness and self-control. Are politically-active Christians known for displaying these tendencies? Ask an irreligious person (especially a politically liberal one) that question, and you're likely get laughed out of the room. We tend to act and speak like everyone else, especially when it comes to politics. And that is a tragedy. Our opponents should be forced to admit, "I don't

agree with those people, but I wish everyone acted the way they do."
Why? Because our ultimate goal, in all we do, should be to glorify God,
not to crush our rivals. That doesn't mean we compromise our
convictions. But it should—at the very least—mean we show them a
different way to live. So, whatever else you take from this chapter, I
hope you and I can agree that we need to pray for a renewing
movement of the Spirit in the American Church. That's what it will
take for the Church to regain its moral credibility.

Watch the news with discernment. If you grew up in
church, like me, you were taught that the media you consume has an
impact on your heart. You may recall the song, "Be careful little eyes
what you see." Even better is the teaching of Jesus in Matthew 6:22-
23: *The eye is the lamp of the body. If your eyes are healthy, your whole body will
be full of light. But if your eyes are unhealthy, your whole body will be full of
darkness. If then the light within you is darkness, how great is that darkness!* This
is why many devout Christians will avoid watching anything that
contains objectionable content. For instance, before I watch a movie,
I check the "parents' guide" on IMDB.com to find out how much
profanity, sex and violence are in it. But many of us have no
restrictions on the amount of news we consume. Some keep their TV
tuned to a 24-hours news channel for virtually every waking hour of
the day. Others check the headlines on their phones any time they have
a spare moment. You may wonder why this would be a problem. After
all, shouldn't we be informed of the events in our world? Absolutely.
But I would argue that undiscerning news consumption can be just as
toxic to the soul as the subversive entertainment we Christians so often
criticize. It increases our levels of anxiety, so that we begin to crave
political Messiahs. It makes us suspicious of our neighbors, and short-
circuits our ability to love them in Christ's name. I believe there are at
least three steps that Christians must take to combat this.

First, we need to recognize the agenda behind the news sources
we consume. By "agenda," I don't mean either a conservative or liberal
slant that a network or website might have, although these days, it's

almost impossible to find a source that even tries to be politically neutral. I mean the true agenda of all media: Money. Whether it's Fox or CNN, The Wall Street Journal or The New York Times, Breitbart or Huffington, these are all businesses, and their income is driven by ratings, subscribers, and web hits. They have all realized that the only way to make us watch, read or click—and keep us coming back—is by showing us the sensational. This is why the focus is on disasters, celebrities, and extreme voices. This is why every story is "breaking news." It's why the news on your Facebook feed keeps talking about the same subjects—their algorithm has figured out what issues you care about, and they keep shoving it in front of you, so you'll keep clicking. When I say, "recognize the agenda," I mean that we must be wise enough to see how these companies try to addict us. I also mean we talk back to ourselves: When we hear a story of tragedy, we mourn and pray, but we also remind ourselves there are good things happening in the world, too. God is real, and His redemption plan is advancing. When we hear a statement from someone on "the other side" that makes us angry, we say, "Yes, but there's probably more to that position than the five-second soundbite gave me, and this guy may not accurately represent them, anyway." I can't tell you how many times I've heard preachers quoted in news stories and wanted to scream out loud, "That guy doesn't speak for me!" And it means knowing when to turn off the TV, close the laptop, or put your phone back in your pocket. Speaking of which…

Second, we need to limit our exposure to the news. In his recent book, *The Wisdom Pyramid: Feeding Your Soul in a Post-truth World*, Brett McCracken reminds us of those "food pyramids" we learned about as kids, which encouraged us to center our diets around vegetables and whole grains, and limit fats and sugars. He said that if we want to grow in wisdom (which is the ability to see the world as God does), we need to do something similar with our media consumption. Scripture is at the foundation of our Wisdom pyramid, followed by the church, nature, good books, and good art. The internet and social media are at the tip of the pyramid, meaning we should consume them the way a healthy person eats dessert. I have made a few changes after reading McCracken's book. I used to look at news headlines on my phone before I even rolled out of bed. Now God's Word is the first thing I read in the morning. I also have a bad habit of opening up Facebook or Twitter whenever I have a spare moment (while standing in line, or between tasks at work). Now, I am trying to check those sites once or twice a day, and to stop using my phone as a distraction from boredom. For those who mainly get their news from TV, I would suggest setting a hard limit: In my opinion, thirty minutes of TV news is more than enough for one person in a typical day. Go for a walk. Talk to your family. Read a good book. There are better, healthier ways to spend your time.

Third, banish "Political entertainment" from your life. By political entertainment, I mean the opinion shows that are on the 24 hour news channels in the evenings. I mean the sarcastic memes that get passed around online. I mean the articles and tweets you can't wait to share, because they so completely "own" the other side. And I mean the videos that feature some guy behind the wheel of his car ranting about how evil and/or stupid "those people" are, or spouting the latest conspiracy theory. Please believe me, I say this out of love for you: Political entertainment is porn for the political idolater. In the same way literal pornography draws us into worshipping sexual gratification, political entertainment feeds the rage and self-righteousness that make us despise our opponents. I'm sure some of you are thinking, "But this is how I know what the other side is up to." That's not true. The perspective these media give you about your opponents is extreme, not accurate. Don't believe me? If you're a conservative, spend some time watching or reading liberal/progressive media. Does it seem to you that they accurately depict the way you and your friends think? Not even close. And conservative media does the same. In fact, many of the people who produce this stuff don't even fully believe it themselves. In the past year, both Fox's Tucker Carlson and MSNBC's Rachel Maddow have successfully defended themselves from defamation lawsuits by essentially arguing, "No one who watches our show should think they're getting the real, objective facts."[xiv] Think about that: These people will tell you what you want to hear, so you'll keep watching. But when their bottom line is at stake, they'll admit they are manipulating you. Turn them off. Your soul will thank you.

Be peacemakers. When we read Jesus' words in the Beatitudes, *Blessed are the peacemakers,* we tend to think of someone who comes between two sworn enemies and brings them together. But there are other ways of making peace. Christians should be the people in society who tamp down hysteria, not the ones who feed it. I see three ways we can do this in our political engagement. First, by treating our opponents the way we want to be treated. 1 Peter 3:15-16 is a well-known passage about defending our faith:

> *But in your hearts honor Christ the Lord as holy, always being prepared to make a defense to anyone who asks you for a reason for the hope that is in you; yet do it with gentleness and respect, having a good conscience, so that, when you are slandered, those who revile your good behavior in Christ may be put to shame.*

Notice that we don't defend our faith by ridiculing their beliefs or attacking their character, but by treating them with gentleness and respect. If that's true in disagreements about the truth of the Gospel, how much more should it apply to something less important (and less certain) like our political views? Of course, we can debate our opponents, and even point out the absurdities of their beliefs, so long as we do it in a way that leaves them feeling respected by us.

Second, we make peace by refusing to join in with the mob. Sociologists have noted that in moments of mob violence, most of the people involved had no prior criminal history. It's common to believe these ordinary people just got "caught up" in the moment, but researchers say the truth is far more disturbing. These people saw an opportunity to do something they've always wanted to do (loot a store, attack someone they hate), this time with no consequences, and the temptation was too great. In other words, mob violence—whether it's a riot, a lynching, or a genocide—simply brings out the dark parts of our character that we usually hide. Social media is a place where mobs—both on the left and the right—seem to rule. That leads seemingly peaceful, responsible people to say hurtful, destructive things or to pass along fake news. This explains why we see people with Scripture passages listed in their profiles using profanity and racist slurs, threatening violence, and spreading destructive conspiracy theories. Being a peacemaker means never saying or posting something that doesn't glorify Jesus.

Third, we take that a step further and confront the mob, even (especially) the mob on our own side. When you see a political ally using toxic language, call them out on it (especially if they claim to be a Christian). If they are sharing memes, videos or "facts" that seem to destroy the other side, ask them where they got their information. If they can't cite a credible news source, suggest that they take the post down. Start with private messages, rather than putting them on blast publically (That's consistent with Christ's own commands about confronting those who sin in Matthew 18). This won't make you very popular, and may lead to some uncomfortable conversations, but it may also lead a brother or sister to repentance. For too long, we have sat idly by as fellow Christians destroyed our witness in the eyes of the lost. It's time to do something about that.

Think biblically, not politically, about the issues. We've invented some unique insults in the political realm. If a Republican politician or member of the conservative media doesn't sufficiently toe the party line, or criticizes a GOP President, they are called a "RINO" (Republican in Name Only). If a black leader or celebrity is judged by liberals to be less militant than he should be on social issues, he's accused of being an "Uncle Tom." There are other, similar terms to describe nearly every political issue. In my opinion, no Christian should ever use these terms, no matter how passionately they may disagree with someone. Here's why: When we use those terms, we're implying that what matters most is loyalty to our party or cause. But what if that person has deeply-held personal principles that lead them to disagree with us? What if they believe that Scripture and the Holy Spirit are compelling them to stand apart from their party on this particular issue? Isn't it courageous for them to stand up for what they believe, rather than blindly do what is politically expedient? I believe we need more leaders with that kind of conviction and courage, not less. We should respect them, even if we disagree with their stand.

Of course, that requires us to admit that sometimes our own party can be wrong. I believe that's a major step we all must take in order to be free from political idolatry. This chapter is already long enough, so I will devote the next chapter to an issue-by-issue look at how we should think biblically about politics. So I'll simply say this: when we find biblical reasons to disagree with our own party, we must respond biblically. That's my next point:

Hold our side accountable. In Old Testament times, Kings of Israel would often surround themselves with prophets to help them understand the will of God. In 1 Kings 22, King Ahab called upon 400 prophets to tell him whether he should go to war against Israel's enemies in Ramoth-Gilead. The prophets agreed that Ahab's army couldn't lose. One even made horns out of iron and said, "With these you will gore the enemy." But godly King Jehoshaphat of Judah knew that these "court prophets" weren't speaking the Word of the Lord, but were instead trying to maintain their cushy position by telling the King what he wanted to hear. He asked, *Is there not here another prophet of the Lord of whom we may inquire?* Ahab, a godless King, said that there was one, *but I hate him, for he never prophesies good concerning me, but evil.* Powerful people don't like to hear the hard truth. We see this also in the story of John the Baptist, who courageously called out King Herod for his sexual immorality…and ended up losing his head for it.

There are still court prophets today. Politicians love to be photographed with famous religious leaders. It's a mutually beneficial relationship, as the politician looks more pious, and the religious leader sees his own fame rise. Every time the preacher is interviewed, he defends the politician against any accusation or criticism. One can't help but think that's the price of maintaining access to the throne. I believe our political system would work better, and our nation would be healthier, if we had fewer court prophets, and more John the Baptists.

But it's not just about asking our celebrity preachers to be boldly prophetic. Christians as a whole should be known as people who courageously confront their own political allies when those allies are in the wrong. In fact, I believe that if you are a Christian, your own political party should find you annoying. Christians who are Democrats should speak out for the sanctity of unborn life and for religious freedom. Christians who are Republicans should insist upon policies that benefit the poor, and confront fellow conservatives who use dehumanizing language to describe immigrants. And all Christians should call for justice against politicians (even those who are "on our side") who are caught lying, are credibly accused of corruption or hypocrisy, or who are exposed as moral frauds. Our non-Christian political teammates will at times hate us for it. But isn't that what the world has always done to prophets?

Be missionaries, not culture warriors. In the 1980s, a new kind of Christian activism arose. Christians who were concerned about issues like the killing of unborn life through abortion, the removal of symbols of faith from the public square, the flouting of biblical morality in popular culture and the breakdown of the traditional family began to unify around these issues to become a voting bloc. The leaders of this movement framed it as a war to take back our culture from the forces of godlessness. Since that time, we have become one of the most powerful voting blocs in our nation. We've developed sophisticated, effective strategies for affecting legislation and the courts. But stop for a moment and ask yourself: Can you point to any way in which our culture is more biblical today than it was forty years ago, when our Culture War began? I can't. To make matters worse, the public perception of Christianity has suffered, too. My own denomination was growing by leaps and bounds in 1980, but today, it is in rapid decline, along with most other American Churches. When researchers talk to young adults who are leaving organized religion in droves, many say it's because "churches are too political." Christian families have seen their own children and grandchildren reject the faith because the anger and self-righteousness produced by our political fervor has drowned out the message of the Gospel. We're losing the Culture War, and we're losing the far more important war for the souls of our neighbors...and even our own families.

I believe that, for the most part, our intentions have been noble. And, I need to say this again—I am not suggesting that we stop advocating for righteousness in the public square. But the problem with framing these issues in war terms is that we begin to see anyone who disagrees with us as an enemy who must be defeated at all costs. Jesus consistently spoke against that way of thinking. These are people for whom He died. We want to destroy them, but He wants to save them. It's time for us to return to our original calling as missionaries. Remember, His last words on earth were, *You shall be my witnesses in Jerusalem, Judea and all Samaria, and to the ends of the earth* (Acts 1:8). He didn't say, "You shall force people to live biblically, whether they want to or not." He called us to be missionaries.

How is a missionary different from a culture warrior? A missionary isn't trying to "take back" his country, because he's an alien here. He is a citizen of Heaven (Philippians 3:19-20) trying to bring a little of that world to his mission field. She doesn't get angry with her neighbors for acting in un-Christian ways; how else do we expect unbelievers to behave? Instead of trying to humiliate his opponents, he seeks to persuade them. That means understanding—even respecting—their way of thinking so fully, he can express their views better than they can. She truly loves them, even if they think she's strange. She's willing to be all things to all people so that by all possible means she might win some (1 Corinthians 9:22).

Here's an example from our past: In the mid-80s, when the Culture War was relatively new, AIDS was one of the biggest stories in the news. There was a widespread fear of this terrible disease, since the details of its transmission were mysterious, and slow, agonizing death seemed certain for all its victims. It was a perfect opportunity for the American Church to display the Gospel in action. In the early centuries of the Church, Christians had stood out from their neighbors during plagues which swept through major cities. The pagans would flee, leaving even their dying loved ones behind, but the Christians would stay, tending the sick at risk of their own lives. What if we had done the same thing during the 1980s? What if we had courageously ministered to AIDS victims when no one else would? Most were homosexuals or IV drug users, people who were very much on the other side of the Culture War. But if we had loved them like Jesus does, how much more receptive to His message would they have been? And what would the reputation of the American Church be today?

We failed. That opportunity is gone, but it won't be the last. The key to doing the right thing next time is in how we see our opponents. It doesn't mean we have to whitewash our disagreements with them. Missionaries have often stood against horrible injustices in the nations where they are called; for instance, the practice of widow-burning was banned in India in 1829 because of the activism of foreign Christian workers. We can fight for the social and political causes that we believe in, but we must prioritize the Gospel. All the legislation and Supreme Court victories in the world won't save a single soul. Elections won't stop the decline of Christianity in our nation. If we continue to idolize political power and demonize the lost, He will reach America in some other way: Perhaps through missionaries from places like China, Sub-Saharan Africa and South America, where the Church hasn't forgotten its true calling. I love the American Church, but I love Jesus more. If we don't repent and experience real revival, this country is better off without us. But I am not thinking in terms of defeat. I believe the day is coming, and hopefully soon, when we cast off the yoke of our false political gods and turn back to our one True King. I am prayerfully looking forward to that day.

Objections

If you've stuck with this chapter so far, thank you. But you probably have some objections to what I've said. I want to address three counter-arguments here, before I close.

Objection #1: The other side is evil. The normal rules don't apply. It's easy for evangelicals like me to point to people and groups on the left who seem to hate us and most of the things we love. Since these people fight dirty, the argument goes, we can't afford to play nice. Loving our neighbor is biblical, of course. But aren't we loving our neighbors when we stand up against those who would overturn the things that make this country a great place to live? After all, if a stranger breaks into your neighbor's home, he would want you to help him defend his family, not invite the invader to church. Don't we have a responsibility to defeat the looming tyranny of liberalism by any means necessary?

The problem with this argument is that I know too many liberals. I disagree with them about many things, but have not found that any of them fit the description above (to clarify again, I am speaking of those I know personally, not the ones I read about in the news or see on social media). Many are non-religious, and some even have a skeptical attitude toward Christianity, but none of them hate Christians. Meanwhile, many others are churchgoing Christians, themselves. In fact, black Christians tend to be politically liberal at roughly the same rate as white evangelicals are politically conservative. In case you think that's evidence that black Christians take their Christian faith less seriously than white ones, the research shows that in nearly every way, the opposite is true. Black Christians are much more likely, on average, to attend church, be part of a small group, read and memorize Scripture, and say that their faith makes a difference in how they live than white Christians.[xv] This tells me that two of our common assumptions are false. One, we assume that our faith guides our voting, and therefore our political views put us on God's side. But since millions of faithful Christians disagree with us, I think it's more likely that we, like all people (black and white, religious and irreligious), tend to vote in a way that benefits us, and then cherry-pick the aspects of our faith that agree with our politics. Our second false assumption is that those radical liberals we see on the news and interact with online are "the true face of the left." I don't believe that's true, any more than I think that white supremacists and Q-Anon believers are the "true face of the right."

Occasionally, a Christian will challenge me with this argument: "Plenty of German pastors were silent when the Nazis took over their country. You should speak out against the evils in the political realm." I agree that pastors should do the work of prophets, showing how Scripture exposes the injustice and wickedness of our culture. But my primary job is to disciple the sheep God has given me. Rather than rail at the sinners outside, I'm called to confront the log in our own eyes. If the day comes when some American politician or party starts putting people on trains to concentration camps, I pray that I and all God's people would stand up against it. But nothing close to that is happening now, and it's intellectually dishonest to imply that it is.

Others ask, "Aren't you worried about the rising popularity of socialism, especially among younger Americans? Don't you find it disturbing how quickly our society has re-written the rules regarding gender and sexuality? Aren't you concerned that someday soon, churches will lose their tax-exempt status, and pastors may even face jail time simply for teaching culturally unpopular Scriptural truths?" Yes, yes and yes. But I also see things happening on the political right that I am convinced make the Lord weep. More importantly, I believe the biggest threat to Christianity in our country is inside the Church, not outside it. If we overcome the idolatry within our own hearts, nothing that happens in Washington—or anywhere else--can stop the people of the Living God.

Objection #2: You just want to be liked by the world. Jesus was clear: *If the world hates you, keep in mind that it hated me first* (John 15:18, NIV). He knew we would be tempted to "fit in" with the world rather than shining as lights in the darkness. All of us should regularly ask ourselves, "Am I motivated by a desire to avoid offending unbelievers for the sake of my own popularity?" That's true in the workplace, the locker room, the university lecture hall, and it's certainly true when we discuss political issues in the public circle. The Holy Spirit knows our true motives, and He can make them known to us, so that we can repent when needed. As for me, I believe that I am genuinely motivated by a desire to see God's people overcome idolatry. I pray that if I'm wrong about that, the Spirit will show me.

Some Christians push the issue further: "Jesus said some really harsh things that made people mad. Isn't it wrong, then, to insist we be kind to people who disagree with us?" Read the Gospels and note who Jesus said harsh things to, and who hated Him. It wasn't sinners, prostitutes and tax collectors. They loved Him. It wasn't Samaritans or pagans, either. It was the religious elites among His own people, the scribes and Pharisees. For the sinners, and even foreigners, He had nothing but kindness. Did He want to be liked by them? Of course not. Jesus wasn't governed by such shallow motives. He loved them and wanted to draw them to Himself, so they could be saved. So why did He speak so brashly to the religious leaders? For the same reason. He loved them, and wanted them to see that they weren't living the righteous lives they thought they were. All of this leads me to believe that if Jesus had come in 21st Century America, He would appeal with great kindness and grace to precisely the kind of people we evangelicals so often consider our enemies. Meanwhile, He would have harsh words for us, because we know the Word, and we're not living it out.

Objection #3: But if we act the way you are advocating, we won't be as powerful. I actually agree with this objection. If evangelical Christians cease voting strictly in our own self-interest; if we start letting Scripture, rather than blind loyalty to our party, dictate our beliefs, words and actions; if we begin to truly love even the people we most fiercely disagree with, we will almost certainly have less influence on future elections. We would have to be naïve to think otherwise. Our political system favors those who do whatever it takes to win. If serving Christ becomes more important to us than wielding power, there will be a price to pay.

So do we trust God or not? We hear the words of Isaiah from 2700 years ago: *If you do not stand firm in your faith, you won't stand at all.* Will we continue to be like feckless, faithless King Ahaz, trusting in political power to be our salvation, or will we follow Jesus, no matter the cost?

Most Christians are familiar with Psalm 46:10: *Be still and know that I am God. I will be exalted among the nations, I will be exalted in the earth.* We often interpret that verse in the context of our frantic lives as if it means, "Stop rushing around, take time to be still and quiet in God's presence." And of course, that's good advice. But it's not what that verse means. In Hebrew, "Be still" means literally "cease striving." The Lord knew that His people were like a kid who needs an injection in order to get well. Rather than sit still, so the doctor can give him the life-saving medicine, the kid will run from her, fearing the pain. When Israel was afraid, they would enslave themselves to a foreign power, or start worshipping the gods of larger nations. These sorts of ideas only got them into deeper trouble. So what God is really saying here is, "Stop trying to fight this battle your way. Let this time of fear drive you closer to me. I will take care of you; let me be God." What happens when we cease striving, and let Him be God? What happens when we let Jesus replace our political gods on the throne of our hearts? That's the beginning of healing. That's when the American Church starts to resemble the Church in Acts: A Spirit-filled, soul-winning, culture-shaking force of God! This uncertain time could be the birthing-room for a revival of God's Church that leads to a new Great Awakening across this land.

You may think that's an impossible dream. You may think our nation is on a downward spiral that cannot be stopped. But let us consider our history for a moment: Imagine you and I could go back in time to speak to those weary, freezing soldiers under George Washington at Valley Forge and tell them that this new nation would still be around more than 2 centuries later, and would be the freest, most prosperous country on Earth. They would think that was too good to be true. Imagine you could speak to Abe Lincoln during the darkest days of the Civil War, and tell him that this nation would indeed come back together in a new birth of freedom. He'd find it hard to accept such hopeful news. Imagine speaking to one of the freedom riders attacked by firehoses and German Shepherds during the Civil Rights Movement, and telling him that his children would someday have equal opportunities with whites. He'd think you were dreaming. During the 1980s, imagine telling someone who'd lived their entire life in the Cold War that the Soviet Union would collapse in less than a decade. They'd tell you to change your medication. God can do far greater things than those. He is the author of the impossible. If we turn back to Christ with all our hearts, He will do abundantly more than we can ask or think. That's what I'm praying for. Won't you join me?

Chapter 10

The Idol of Politics Part II: Thinking Biblically

In the previous chapter, I asserted that one way to overcome political idolatry is to think biblically, not politically, about the issues. But how do we do that? In my opinion, our churches have done a fine job of teaching us how to be church members. They've even taught us biblical principles for marriage, parenting, money management, and a host of other life skills. But they haven't trained us to apply the Scriptures to the contentious issues of our day. As a pastor, I understand why. God's Word is absolute truth, and if we preach it faithfully, it steps on people's toes. Generally speaking, most churchgoers are willing—even eager--to be challenged about the way they live, but not the way they vote. As a result, many pastors tend to avoid Scriptural teachings that infringe too painfully on the political beliefs of their parishioners.

So now watch a fool like me rush in where angels fear to tread. I don't claim to be the world's authority on these subjects. At the end of this chapter, I'll suggest some authors who do a much better job of analyzing the issues. But I hope this can serve as a starting point, an example of how one Christian applies God's Word to these difficult questions. My hope is that, where you think I have handled Scripture correctly, you will allow it to renew your mind, so that from now on, you approach all issues more biblically than before. My prayer is that we will stop allowing the loudest, most extreme voices on the political landscape tell us what to believe, since we have God's inspired Word in our hands. I pray that we will become the people least likely to fall for misinformation, spin, and absurd conspiracy theories. Most of all, I pray that we will shine like lights in a divisive culture, boldly speaking the truth in love, offending people (on both sides) with that truth when necessary, but consistently, unimpeachably fighting for the good of others. In other words, I pray that we would act like Jesus in the political realm. Someone certainly needs to.

Here is my attempt to think biblically on the following issues:

Abortion

A non-Christian asked me once why we care so much about abortion. My answer was that this is the rare political cause that seems to be unquestionably righteous (at least in our eyes). Like most other people, we know deep down that we tend to vote in a self-interested way. We are most passionate about causes that impact us directly, most supportive of measures that will make our lives more comfortable. But when it comes to abortion, Christians feel we are standing up for someone else. We're fighting for the rights of a group (pre-born babies) who cannot defend themselves. While so many political issues seem gray and complicated, this one seems black-and-white. Does Scripture agree?

The word "abortion" does not appear in the Bible. But God's feelings about pre-born children certainly do. Perhaps the most well-known example is Psalm 139:13-16, where the Psalmist writes,

For you created my inmost being; you knit me together in my mother's womb. I praise you because I am fearfully and wonderfully made; your works are wonderful, I know that full well. My frame was not hidden from you when I was made in the secret place, when I was woven together in the depths of the earth. Your eyes saw my unformed body; all the days ordained for me were written in your book before one of them came to be.

In Jeremiah 1:5, God tells the prophet:

Before I formed you in the womb I knew you, and before you were born I consecrated you; I appointed you a prophet to the nations.

In Luke 1:41-44, the first human being to recognize Jesus' divinity is a baby in the womb of his mother, as pre-born John the Baptist leaps inside Elizabeth when he hears the voice of Mary for the first time.

If God knows us before we're born, if He meticulously fashions us in our mother's womb, if He has our whole lives planned out for us before we ever breathe on our own, then clearly He sees us as human. Psalm 106:38-39 shows how angry God felt toward His people when they sacrificed their own children to their idols, polluting the land with innocent blood. It's logical to believe that He feels the same way when we end the lives of our children before they have the opportunity to live out His wonderful plans for them.

The question then becomes, "At what point is the unborn baby a human life?" The answer for many is viability, which is another way of saying, "The fetus is a human life when it's able to survive outside the womb." Of course, with the advancement of medical technology, the age of viability keeps changing. In 2020, a little boy named Curtis Means was born in Alabama at only 21 weeks of gestation. My question is, why is the burden of proof on the pre-born child to "prove" he is human? Why not assume every fetus, at every stage of development, is a person until we know otherwise? Why are we drawing seemingly arbitrary lines when it comes to something as precious as human life? In short, based on Scripture and basic biology, I believe a righteous and just society will do whatever can be done to ensure that every pre-born child has a chance at life.

That's the black-and-white of abortion, in my opinion. Now it gets complicated.

Should exceptions be made for women who are raped or are the victims of incest? I would never dismiss or attempt to minimize the horrific trauma that would accompany bringing such a child to term. But in the end, it's still a child. Does that child not also deserve a chance for life? Shouldn't a righteous society focus on finding ways to bring such children into the world in a way more supportive of both mother and baby? Only about 1.5% of abortions are sought because of rape or incest[xvi], so even if we make exceptions in these cases, this is certainly not a reason to protect all abortion on demand. What about cases in which carrying a child to term will endanger the life of the mother, or situations of profound deformity in which, if the baby even survives delivery, it will die within minutes or hours? Should women in such situations be forced to deliver? These are certainly not easy questions. Some Christians support allowing the option of abortion in such cases, while praying that medical technology would advance to the point that such cases, already extremely rare, would be a thing of the past. Others believe that, even in such cases, we have no right to prioritize the mental and physical health of the mother over that of her child.

How do we protect the life of the unborn? For most of my life, the answer from the pro-life side has focused on legislation and the courts: Capture statehouses, and urge representatives to pass laws that restrict abortion. Elect Presidents who will appoint Supreme Court justices who will then overturn Roe v. Wade, the 1973 ruling that made abortion legal in the first place. In light of Scripture, a ruling that prioritizes a "right to privacy" over the life of a child is indeed evil, and therefore these political efforts are worthy. But overturning Roe v. Wade won't end abortion in America. It will merely allow individual states to make their own abortion laws. One study found that if Roe v. Wade were overturned, it would only reduce abortions by 13%.[xvii] And even if the pro-life movement were able to ban abortion in all fifty states, thousands of abortions would still take place each year. So when the day comes that Roe v. Wade is overturned, we shouldn't celebrate as if the battle is won. It's only getting started.

How do I know this? The abortion rate has been declining in

America for over forty years, and today it's actually lower than it was in 1973, the year of Roe v. Wade. That's right, women were more likely to obtain abortions before the procedure was legal than they are today. In other words, changing the law won't change the fact that many women who are pregnant do not feel they can bring their baby to term. If abortion is banned, many will still find a way to terminate their pregnancies. To truly be pro-life, we cannot simply ban abortion. We must seek to end it.

How? I think the answer requires asking other questions, such as: What factors have caused the abortion rate to decline? What factors drive women to seek abortions in the first place? Obviously, if we want to save unborn lives, we should work to accentuate the first set of factors, while addressing the second set. What about the men involved in these pregnancies? Could tougher laws against deadbeat dads reduce the number of abortions? Of course, we know the answers to those questions will vary, depending on the source. Conservatives will say that the ultimate answer is to strengthen families, while maintaining a healthy overall economy. These should be supplemented by supporting adoption, foster families, and the work of crisis pregnancy centers. Progressives will point to initiatives such as more access to contraceptives, free child care, and an increase in the child tax credit. Thinking biblically instead of politically means being willing to try any solution--even those that don't fit with our own political ideals—that saves lives. Are we as evangelicals willing to support all proposals that will reduce the number of abortions, even if some of those proposals seem "liberal"? If not, then we're guided by political idolatry, not our Scriptural convictions.

Racial equality

In the 1990s, the Promise Keepers movement packed stadiums

full of men who pledged before God to be better husbands, fathers, church members and citizens. By 1996, the leaders of the movement, spurred by founder Bill McCartney, decided to turn the focus of their rallies toward the sixth of their seven promises: to work towards racial reconciliation. According to a recent article, McCartney was "...convicted that racism was a great sin and that the church was responsible for letting the cultural division continue. He believed it grieved God and that no movement—no Christian endeavor—would prosper unless racial reconciliation was a priority."[xviii]

A quarter-century later, as protests and riots engulfed several US cities in the wake of the George Floyd and Ahmaud Arberry murders, many evangelicals blamed rhetoric from the political left, particularly the influence of Critical Race Theory, for the national division around race. Yet instead of responding with our own, more Gospel-centered plan for racial equality and peace, this time the response was to shut down any talk about racism at all. In this new day, any preacher, Christian author or podcaster who shows sympathy for the anger and sorrow of racial minorities in America is in danger of being branded "woke." I would argue instead that caring about racial equality is biblical. Consider:

Genesis 1:27 tells us that God created humans in His image. That means all humans, not just those of a particular race, bear the image of God, and are precious to Him.

In Numbers 12, Moses is publicly criticized by his siblings Aaron and Miriam for marrying a Cushite woman (Cush was a part of Africa, and Cushites were black). The voice of God thundered forth, defending Moses, and cursing Aaron and Miriam.

In Jeremiah 38, an Ethiopian named Ebed-Melech rescues the prophet Jeremiah, who has been left to die in a muddy well by the servants of Judah's King, Zedekiah. God declares that Ebed-Melech will survive the Babylonian invasion, but the King and his servants, although members of the "chosen people," will not.

The genealogy of Jesus found in Matthew 1 features four women, three of whom are non-Jewish (Tamar, Rahab and Ruth). Rahab, a former prostitute from Jericho, is even listed among the heroes of faith in Hebrews 11. And Ruth has an entire book of the Bible devoted to her story, in which we discover that this Moabite becomes the great-grandmother of King David.

Jesus often confronted racial prejudice. In His sermon in the Nazareth synagogue (Luke 4), He reminds the citizens of His hometown that in the days of Elijah and Elisha, God reserved His greatest miracles for non-Jews. They become enraged at this and try to kill Him. Often, He leads His disciples to the other side of the Sea of Galilee, which was Gentile territory, for healing and preaching. When a teacher of the Law asks Jesus who is covered by the command to "love your neighbor as yourself" in Leviticus, He responds with the story of a Samaritan who helps an injured Jew, after a priest and a Levite pass him by. The hatred between Jews and Samaritans at that time was so intense, the crowds must have been shocked at the parable. In His view, every human is our neighbor. Jesus also leads a Samaritan woman to salvation, then spends several days in her town, making believers of most of the population (John 4).

We see a stunning series of events in three consecutive chapters of Acts. First, in chapter 8, Philip begins evangelizing the Samaritans, who respond so enthusiastically, the apostles send Peter and John to investigate. In the midst of this spiritual harvest, God calls Philip to leave for the desert road near Gaza, where he meets an Ethiopian official and leads him to Christ. In chapter 9, Jesus appears to a racially proud terrorist named Saul of Tarsus, and changes his life so significantly, he becomes the evangelist to the non-Jewish world. Then in chapter 10, Peter preaches to a house full of Gentiles at the home of Cornelius, all of whom come into the family of faith. But this only happens after God shows Peter in a dream that racial distinctions are irrelevant.

Paul didn't just want to bring Gentiles to Christ; He wanted to heal racial division. In Ephesians 2:11-22, he speaks of God's "mystery" (his secret plan) to destroy racism through creating a new temple, with Jesus as the cornerstone, made up of different races worshipping together in love and unity. It all leads to a beautiful vision of our future, where people of every nation, race, tribe and tongue will worship King Jesus together on the New Earth (Revelation 7). The message is clear: If we harbor any racial prejudice, we are not living for Christ.

Of course, none of these Scriptures endorse any specific political initiatives to bring about racial equality. Scripture doesn't tend to focus on legislation, instead showing us what God cares about and trusting us to use God-given wisdom to find solutions to the problems that break His heart. So it's not unbiblical to find fault with laws or policies that attempt to bring about equality in ways that will have unintended consequences that are even worse. The question is, "What solutions do we offer?" Whether you and I are progressive or conservative politically, the Bible is clear: We should be part of the solution to the racial divide in our nation. At the very least, we Christians should be the first to listen when our neighbors of other races are telling us, "Things aren't right."

The fact is, many members of racial minority groups—and particularly black Americans—have a very different experience of this country than we who are white. While America is still the land of opportunity (enough so that millions of people still want to immigrate here), history shows a series of policies and systems that disadvantaged black Americans. As a result, the average black child starts out life with challenges that my kids—and most other white children—never had to face. For just one example, for many decades, most black Americans could not buy homes in good neighborhoods, thanks to policies like redlining. Home ownership is one of the main ways a person accumulates wealth. Little wonder, then, that today, one in three black families have zero or negative wealth. Where opportunities for advancement are lacking, people tend to turn to crime. So it's not surprising that one in three black men born in 2001 will spend time in prison at some point in their lives. There are other, equally heartbreaking statistics where those came from.[xix]

To put it in terms of our Lord's parable, our neighbor is bleeding. Will we walk past him? Will we blame him for traveling a dangerous road on his own? Or will we find ways to help him up? I don't know the solutions. But I do know that refusing to listen to our black neighbors when they cry out is not the way of Jesus. We must care. And the world should see that we care, or they will rightly conclude that the love of God is not in us.

Gender and sexuality

Over the past twenty years, the way Americans think about sexual identity and gender has changed so rapidly and dramatically, it has left even some mainstream media members astonished. For instance, in 2004, nearly two-thirds of Americans opposed gay marriage. Just fifteen years later, the percentages had flipped, with 61% of Americans supporting gay marriage, and only 31 percent opposing it.[xx] Meanwhile, 62% of Americans reported being more supportive of transgender rights than they were five years ago.[xxi] These revised attitudes have impacted our social landscape in a variety of ways. For instance, major corporations, including professional sports leagues, now frequently boycott states that are perceived to be unfriendly to gay or transgender rights. Gay marriage has been legal in the US since 2015, with the Supreme Court's Obergfell v. Hodges ruling. And the US House of Representatives in 2019 passed The Equality Act for the first time. It failed to pass the Senate, but advocates will continue to press for its passage in future sessions. If passed as currently written, churches and religious organizations will no longer be allowed to appeal to freedom of religion when confronted with accusations of discrimination on the basis of sexual orientation or gender identity. In plain English, that means that faith-based hospitals and insurers could be forced to provide gender-transition therapies, faith-based schools and universities could be forced to permit homosexual acts in their codes of conduct, and churches could be forced to rent their facilities for same-sex marriages.

What does the Bible say about these issues? Let's start with three Scriptural truths:

1) God created sex to be shared within marriage between a man and a woman. Any other expression of sexual intercourse is outside His will for our lives.

2) Homosexual activity is not a major topic within the pages of Scripture, but where it is mentioned, it is condemned without exception.

3) God created two genders, male and female, and declared a gender binary humanity to be "very good." In the only Scriptural reference to gender non-conformity, God condemns such behavior (Deuteronomy 22:5).

Some Christians from more theologically liberal traditions would dispute the three points above. I don't have space in this chapter to interact with their arguments. If you are interested, there are several good resources to consult. Here are four I recommend: *Embodied: Transgender Identities, The Church, and What the Bible Has to Say*, by Preston Sprinkle; *The Secular Creed: Engaging Five Contemporary Claims*, by Rebecca McLaughlin, and *The Coming Tsunami* and *7 Critical Issues*, by Jim Denison. But let's look at how thinking biblically will lead us to critique both the left and the right.

The political left would say that biblical teaching on these issues is no different from the rhetoric of some preachers in the past who used Scripture to justify slavery and racial discrimination. Some even say, "The God you believe in hates people who are gay or gender non-binary." To this, I say two things: First of all, it is the political idolatry of the American Church that has produced that argument. We have no one but ourselves to blame. I will defend that point a little later.

Second, the Bible itself would fiercely disagree. 1 Corinthians 6:9-11 says, *⁹ Or do you not know that the unrighteous will not inherit the kingdom of God? Do not be deceived: neither the sexually immoral, nor idolaters, nor adulterers, nor men who practice homosexuality, ¹⁰ nor thieves, nor the greedy, nor drunkards, nor revilers, nor swindlers will inherit the kingdom of God. ¹¹ And such were some of you. But you were washed, you were sanctified, you were justified in the name of the Lord Jesus Christ and by the Spirit of our God.* Paul personally knew the people to whom he was writing in that letter. He's not being rhetorical. He's saying, "Before you met Jesus, some of you used to be ruled by an addiction to alcohol. Some used to be ruled by an insatiable desire for money. Some of you used to be ruled by your sexual desire for people of the opposite gender. And some of you used to be ruled by your sexual desire for people of your own gender." But notice what he says next: "But you were washed, you were sanctified, you were justified in the name of Jesus."

Notice that he doesn't condemn the homosexual members of the Corinthian church for their sexual orientation, any more than he condemns the alcoholic members for having a taste for wine, or the greedy members for their desire to have nice things. I have known many people who were attracted to people of their own sex. None of them chose that orientation. Some, who were Christians, wished they could change. Paul is absolutely not saying that God was angry with them because of the way they were born. He does say, "That's not who you are anymore. This stuff doesn't separate you from God anymore, because you've been justified. It doesn't rule your life anymore, because you've been sanctified." Far from hating gay people, Christ loves them enough to die for them. He loves them enough to offer them a new life. That doesn't mean He promises to change their orientation, any more than he promises all alcoholics that they will never feel a desire for liquor again. I am aware of same-sex attracted Christians who, over time, became attracted to members of the opposite sex. But that is not the experience of the same-sex attracted Christians I know personally. Instead, they have chosen to live celibate lives. They find—like Paul himself--that the love of Jesus is indeed enough. In the same way, God loves people who experience gender dysphoria. He wants to show them how to live an abundant life. While the prevailing idea these days is that such people should embrace a new identity, including gender transition therapies, the biblical view would insist that the only "new identity" which will truly fulfill them is found in Christ.

Some may wonder, "Why does God care so much about this? Why doesn't He let consenting adults follow the desires that bring them pleasure?" Unlike other religions, Christianity isn't merely a list of rules and rituals that enable us to earn our way into Heaven. We are saved because of what Jesus did for us on the cross, not because of anything we can do. So the commands in the Bible exist not in order to earn God's love, but because God already loves us and wants what's best for us. His rules aren't intended to make our lives difficult; they are given to bring us joy, to spare us pain. Imagine you lived in a world where the dangers of smoking were unknown. You would tell people, "God didn't create our lungs to breathe in tobacco smoke." Your opponents would point to dozens of people they knew who smoked without showing any signs of ill health. This, in their view, would prove that we were wrong, and that smoking was harmless. But you and I both know that it would prove no such thing. In the same way, many have rejected the biblical views of sexuality and gender because they have met people in loving homosexual relationships, and transgendered people who seem happy in their transition. As Christians, we must graciously hold onto God's design for sexuality and gender, knowing that ultimately, abandoning that design produces devastating harm.

Now let's look at the rhetoric on this issue from the Christian political right. There, we are told that issues of sexuality and gender are the key battleground issues of our times. "The more we give in on these issues, the more likely it is that God will judge our nation," they say. Therefore, we cannot afford to show empathy or respect for those who disagree with us, but must treat them like enemies in a war, who must be defeated at all costs. Some cite the story of Sodom and Gomorrah in Genesis 19. God had decided to destroy those two cities, but He sent two angels into Sodom to rescue Abraham's nephew Lot before the fire from Heaven started. The two angels looked like ordinary men, and soon a gang of locals surrounded Lot's house, looking to rape them. So the argument goes, "See, God hates homosexuality so much, He'd destroy whole cities for it." But that's not actually the reason why God destroyed those cities. Ezekiel 16:49 tells us the real reason: *Now this was the sin of your sister Sodom: She and her daughters were arrogant, overfed and unconcerned; they did not help the poor and needy.*

There is a long, sad history of religious folks becoming hyper-focused on sexual sins, treating them as if they are a special category of evil, worse than more pedestrian flaws like gossiping or greed. It was even that way in Jesus' time. For just one example, think about the sinful woman who anointed Jesus with oil at Simon the Pharisee's house (Luke 7:36-50). Simon despised this woman for her lifestyle, but Jesus said, "She loves me more than you do, because unlike you, she's been forgiven." To assume that God is angry about America's sexual permissiveness but doesn't care about issues like racial equality is to think more like the Pharisees than like Jesus. When I said earlier that the American Church's political idolatry has produced the idea that our God hates gay and non-binary people, this is what I mean: In my experience, most Christians are kind, loving, accepting people who don't hate anyone. But we gained this reputation because, somewhere along the way, we stopped reaching out to people like the sinful woman in Luke 7 and prioritized the political debates around sexuality and gender. We stopped trying to reconcile people to God because we were too focused on trying to win an argument in our culture.

Am I concerned about the religious liberty implications I spoke of earlier, including the Equality Act? Of course. But I am more concerned about the souls of men and women who will never give the Gospel a hearing because they believe our God hates them. I vote for leaders who support religious freedom, but not for those who use inflammatory and sensationalistic language against those with whom we disagree. No disciple of Jesus should ever use such language, or participate in cruel joking about this community. In fact, we should be the first to repudiate those who do. On a more personal level, Christians who have friends or family members who are gay or non-binary should stop arguing with them and simply love them the way Jesus loves us (I mentioned Preston Sprinkle's book *Embodied* earlier, and it's an excellent resource for Christians on how to love transgendered people without compromising biblical truth). Remember: It's not our job to change their behavior. It's our job to bring them to Jesus. He'll take care of the rest.

Poverty/Immigration

There is no political issue that Scripture addresses more often than that of poverty. The poor are mentioned over 2000 times in the Bible. For instance:

I know that the Lord will maintain the cause of the afflicted, and will execute justice for the needy. Psalm 140:12

Whoever is generous to the poor lends to the LORD, and he will repay him for his deed. Proverbs 19:17

But if anyone has the world's goods and sees his brother in need, yet closes his heart against him, how does God's love abide in him? 1 John 3:17

We have already seen from Ezekiel 16 that God destroyed the cities of Sodom and Gomorrah for lacking compassion for the poor. When you read the other prophets (especially Amos), you see that God judges a nation that doesn't take care of her poorest citizens. The same is true for immigrants. Throughout the Old Testament, we read of God's special concern for three groups: Widows, orphans and immigrants. Why? Because these were the people with the least power and privilege. God often reminded the Israelites that they had been immigrants in Egypt, so they should treat foreigners in their own land with great hospitality (See Exodus 22:21, Leviticus 19:33-34, Deuteronomy 10:18-19, among many others). I included immigrants and the poor in the same category because they represent those whom Jesus called, "The least of these" in His parable of the sheep and the goats (Matthew 25:40). In that parable, Jesus says His true people will be marked not merely by religious devotion and moral uprightness, but by their compassion for those at the bottom of society.

Christians on the political right would argue that such Scriptures call for charity on the part of churches and individual Christians, but not for specific government programs, which may have unintended consequences that end up making the lives of the poor worse. To their credit, conservatives on average give more to charity than their liberal counterparts.[xxii] But there are commands in the Law of Moses (which functioned in many ways like the constitution of political Israel) governing relief for the poor. For instance, in the law of gleaning (Leviticus 19:9-10) landowners were required to leave some of their crop in the fields at harvest time, so that the landless poor could provide for themselves. In a way, it was "work-fare" instead of welfare. The Jubilee law in Leviticus 25 commanded that twice a century, slaves would be set free, debts would be forgiven, and land that had been repossessed would revert to the families that lost it. This way, those who had fallen into poverty could have a new start, and no one could get permanently wealthy from the misfortunes of others.

Similarly, Scripture doesn't contain direct instruction on how many immigrants to allow into one's nation. It does acknowledge that nations have a responsibility to protect their citizens (For instance, God called Nehemiah to rebuild Jerusalem's wall). One can make a plausible argument that restrictions on immigration are necessary not only to keep out evil-doers, but to prevent social safety nets from being overwhelmed. At the very least, however, Scripture commands us to treat the immigrants who are already here with kindness. God is not talking about offering the poor and the immigrant merely enough to keep from starving, either. In Deuteronomy 15:4, God promised the people that if they followed His Law 'there will be no poor among you." A righteous society will seek to lift the poor out of their poverty, to break generational cycles that keep people stuck in frustration and lack of opportunity.

Ironically, conservative Christians sometimes argue the opposite, implying that any attempts to stamp out poverty are doomed to fail, or even unbiblical, since Jesus said, "The poor you will always have with you." But that's not what Jesus meant. Reading that quote in context (Matthew 26:6-13), we see that a woman has just anointed Jesus with outrageously expensive perfume (this is a different incident from the one at Simon the Pharisee's house, in Luke 7). The disciples criticize her wastefulness, saying the perfume could have been sold and given to the poor. Jesus reminds them that they will have the opportunity to help poor people for the rest of their lives, but He will be with them for only a short time. This woman has done the right thing in honoring Jesus while she could. To look at it another way, Scripture clearly indicates that, until Christ returns, there will always be sin on earth. By the logic we use regarding "the poor you will always have among you," that would mean we should not address sin. No Christian I know believes that. Let's not use one saying of Jesus—taken out of context, no less—to override the thousands of biblical commands to take care of the poor.

While I can't make a Scriptural argument for specific proposals or policies regarding "the least of these," here's what I can say for certain that Christians should do:

1) Every local church should be aware of the problems poor people and immigrants face in their community, and should offer programs that address those problems, or partner with local organizations that do. The Church should be known in every city as the people who care.

2) We should be the first to speak out against, and seek to repeal, policies that increase poverty (such as mass incarceration, for instance) or make it harder for poor people to improve their circumstances. We should vote for leaders who offer real solutions to help those who are struggling. Psalm 31:8-9 tells us: *Speak up for those who have no voice, for the justice of all who are dispossessed. Speak up, judge righteously, and defend the cause of the oppressed and needy* (HCSB).

3) We should demand that our leaders find an immigration policy that balances border security with compassion. We should loudly denounce any rhetoric that demonizes immigrants.

Knowing the difference

There are of course scores of issues I haven't even touched on. I encourage you to read the works of writers who thoughtfully apply Scripture to current events and debates, and who have the courage to disagree with both political parties when they are in the wrong. Here are some I have learned from: David French, Karen Swallow Prior, Russell Moore, Jim Denison, Tony Evans, Rod Dreher, among others. Each has written things that I disagreed with at times. My point is not, "Find a guru who will tell you how to vote." But instead, allow thoughtful Christians to help you learn the difference between blind loyalty to a political side (which is idolatry) and thoughtful, Scriptural engagement with the issues.

Meanwhile, work on knowing the difference between the

things you **know** (because they are explicitly Scriptural) and the things you merely **believe** to be true. For instance, I know from Scripture that God hates abortion, racism, sexual immorality, and injustice against the poor. I have beliefs about what should be done on each of those issues, but they are merely my beliefs, not the express will of God.

I know that God expects me to respect and pray for my President and other leaders. I don't know how He feels about their job performance. This is why, as a pastor, I never endorse political candidates. When I preach, the people should expect for me to say only that which I can defend biblically. At times, I have very strong feelings about a political leader. But God knows more than I do. If I tell my church to vote for Candidate A, and he later reveals himself to be a snake in the grass, why should anyone listen to me about anything else? I am quite sure that no Hebrew priest in 605 AD told his people that the Babylonian King Nebuchadnezzar was going to be used powerfully by God to accomplish His will, but that's exactly what happened (see Daniel 4). We should do our best to assess all candidates by their personal character as well as their stand on the issues, but in the end, we should admit that there is much we don't know.

I am a gun owner and believe in the right of individual Americans to bear arms. I cannot claim to know from Scripture how God feels about that. However, I know He hates the amount of gun violence in our nation, and so I should urge our leaders to find ways to prevent it.

I love my country, and believe that those who serve the nation should be honored. But I know that in Scripture, God was critical of the nation He founded (Israel) when she went astray, as she often did. So biblical patriotism is not an unquestioning idealizing of one's nation, but a willingness to hold her accountable to her own ideals.

I know that God has created this world, and has given humanity dominion over it. Therefore, we are responsible for stewarding the environment well. However, I also know that human beings are made in the image of God, and therefore take precedence over other creatures. How should we balance those two truths? How can we take good care of the animal and plant life of the earth without inhibiting the human economies that enable people to flourish? I have beliefs about that, but my opinions are not equal to the Word of God.

Why is this important? If we can't distinguish between the things we believe and the things we know, we will treat every political question as a life-and-death struggle. If we let our political beliefs dictate the way we read Scripture, instead of the other way around, we are guilty of political idolatry. We may win a debate once in a while, but we won't glorify God. And the people God has entrusted to us will be turned away from the salvation that He died to offer them. Pray for wisdom and humility to think biblically about politics. And remember—always remember—our ultimate King is coming. We put our hope in Him, and Him alone. Someday, we will live under the reign of One who governs with perfect justice, righteousness and love; One who never made a self-interested decision in His earthly life; who cared nothing for opinion polls, but cared infinitely for the souls of all human beings. On the day His reign begins, we will finally see the foolishness of our political idolatries. After all, our True King is not an elephant or a donkey. He's a Lamb.

Epilogue: Forever Free

On January 1, 1863, Abraham Lincoln signed a document that said that all slaves residing in Confederate States "shall be then, thenceforward, and forever free." Historians note that the Emancipation Proclamation didn't actually free anyone from slavery. If the Union had lost the Civil War, its high-minded words would have been irrelevant. And it took the passage of the 13th Amendment two years later to make slavery officially illegal in this country. But from the time those words "forever free" echoed across this land, things began to change for millions of Americans. Slaves fled their bondage, now that they knew the Government would no longer send them back to their masters. Many aided the effort to win the victory. Almost two hundred thousand, in fact, fought in black regiments for the Union.

Ironically, freedom didn't immediately make life better for many slaves. Most couldn't read or manage money. Those were among hundreds of life skills they had to learn on the fly. Meanwhile, they faced a world full of barriers. Unjust laws meant that for black people, getting a job, buying a home, or sending their kids to school were nearly impossible. It would take years (in many cases, generations) of persistence and hard work to gain even the most basic aspects of the American Dream. But the starting point, the most non-negotiable step to real freedom, was leaving their masters and never going back.

We too have been freed from bondage. Our freedom didn't come at the stroke of a president's pen or the victory of an army, but at the heroic, sacrificial death of Jesus. Colossians 2:15 puts it this way: *And having disarmed the powers and authorities, he made a public spectacle of them, triumphing over them by the cross* (NIV). Like those slaves, we need to learn new skills in order to fully enjoy our freedom; attributes like loving our neighbor, dying to self, and living a life of worshipful service to God just don't come naturally to us. And the world, the flesh, and the Devil himself are standing in our way, hoping to keep us mired in our pre-conversion misery. But only one thing can actually stop us: Failing to leave our old masters behind. The "powers and authorities" Jesus defeated through His death on the cross include the objects of our false worship. If we hear the Gospel and respond joyfully, but keep on living under the bondage of idolatry, we make a mockery of Christ's sacrifice...and we live as tragic fools, like slaves who've been emancipated but never live in freedom.

But it's even worse than that. When God's people continue to live in idolatry, it keeps others from coming to the God who loves them. We've already seen how, in the Old Testament, God called Israel "a Kingdom of priests" (Exodus 19:6), meaning that, in the same way the priests in the temple were supposed to help the people get right with God, Israel was intended to show the world the blessings of a life free from idols, following the One True God. But the people of God didn't do it. Many an Israelite prayed to God, learned the Torah, and offered sacrifices in the Temple. But he also went to the shrine of Baal on the hill just outside his town, and had a little statue of Asherah in his house. He might participate in the sexual rituals of the gods of his pagan neighbors; after all, they were a lot more enjoyable than the feasts of Jerusalem. And when things got really desperate, he might offer one of his children to Molech. Better to lose one child than to have the entire family die in a plague or famine, he would tell himself. Is it any wonder that Israel never fulfilled their calling to be "a light to the nations" (Isaiah 49:6)? When we go back to the gods Jesus died to free us from, we are following in the footsteps of Old Testament Israel. No matter how doctrinally correct and morally upright we are, if we live with the same fear, anger and selfishness as most people, why would they leave their gods for ours?

On the other hand, imagine what happens when a struggling unbeliever meets someone who:

- Is content with the money and possessions she has, even if it's not great riches.

- If single, is happy and fulfilled in his singleness. If married, is faithful and loving to his spouse.

- Experiences as much pain as everyone else, but doesn't become self-pitying. Forgives those who hurt him and treats with grace those who are difficult to like.

- Doesn't seek attention, and isn't obsessed with impressing others.

- Loves her family deeply, but isn't overwhelmed when her family life gets complicated.

- Is outspoken about his faith in Christ in a way that is compelling, not self-righteous.

- Speaks about political matters graciously, but with a thoughtfulness and wisdom that puts to shame those who are bombastic on the left and the right.

When we live forever free from our idols, we not only experience life as it was meant to be lived, free from the toxic byproducts of our false devotion, we also draw others to salvation. Like freed slaves who have built new lives, we call out to those still in slavery, "It doesn't have to be this way. Look at me!" Our freedom literally helps set others free.

So what would it take for us to live idol-free lives? Here are three things that I believe would change everything, if we only practice them consistently.

Repentance. Millions of people have attended twelve-step programs to help them overcome addictions to alcohol, drugs, and destructive behaviors. Thanks to the movies, the first of the twelve steps is fairly well known: "I admit that I am powerless over alcohol, and my life has become unmanageable." Or as we popularly paraphrase it: In order to get better, we first must admit we have a problem. The originators of the twelve steps were Christians, and brought their biblical understanding of discipleship to addiction recovery. In biblical discipleship, change requires repentance. When we come to the point of desperation, ready to cry out to God for transformation, that's when growth begins. Here's another way to look at it: A married couple might survive one spouse's infidelity, but only if that spouse breaks off the affair. That's an even better illustration of my point, since the Old Testament prophets often compared the idolatry of God's people to marital adultery. Some of those passages are so graphic in their depictions of the people's unfaithfulness, they are difficult to read, even in our sexually explicit age (Ezekiel 23 is one example). The images are shocking for a reason: God wanted His people to know how deeply they were hurting Him. He pleaded with them to confront their unfaithfulness, so that there could be healing.

My prayer for this book is that everyone who reads it would have the insight and honesty to identify their own idols and name them before God. Have you done that yet? Perhaps you can honestly say, "I am fully committed to my Lord. Nothing in my life comes ahead of Him." If so, hallelujah! But hopefully, as you've read these chapters, you've detected the counterfeit gods that compete for your affections, the things that will gladly steal the throne of your heart if you let down your guard. So please, stop reading for a moment, and pray to the Lord, naming your idols specifically before Him. Ask Him to help you put these false gods in their proper place, and keep them there. And remember, repentance isn't a beginning. It's a lifestyle. You and I will be fighting this battle until the day we see Him face to face (more on that later). Don't give up the fight!

Worship: I remember the point in our wedding when the doors of the sanctuary opened, and Carrie stood there in her wedding dress, on the arm of her father. If at that moment, someone had sidled up to me wanting to talk about sports, movies, or history—all subjects that I ordinarily find interesting—I would have ignored them. Heck, if someone had shouted, "The building is on fire!" I wouldn't have flinched. I had only one thing on my mind at that moment, and nothing else held interest for me.

When we truly worship God, we experience something similar to that moment in my wedding, only it's even more profound. As we gain a ravishing vision of how wonderful our Savior is, other things that tend to compete for our allegiance just aren't as compelling anymore. As the old song says,

"Turn your eyes upon Jesus. Look full in His wonderful face.

And the things of earth will grow strangely dim in the light of His glory and grace."

So a key part of overcoming idolatry is learning how to truly worship God. Dean Inserra says, "Sunday morning church is a Saturday night decision." He's right. We must decide before Sunday comes that we are committed to being among God's people in His house. But worship is more than just showing up in the sanctuary. Prepare your heart to enter God's presence long before you walk through the doors of your church. Ask the Spirit to bless your pastor and other worship leaders. Ask Him to give you ears to hear whatever He is saying to you, the ability to focus on the words you are singing, and eyes to see the people around you who need comfort, encouragement, a warm greeting, or an after-service lunch invitation. And pray for others who will be there, that they will connect with God as well.

If we want to live forever free, we can't limit ourselves to worshipping God on Sundays alone. Worship is anything we do that focuses our attention and our affections fully on God. Depending on your personality, there are any number of ways for you to worship throughout the week. For some people, studying Scripture and theology is how they experience His presence. For others, it happens most naturally through silent contemplation. For still others, it's music, nature, or serving those in need that furnishes that connection with the Divine. Find your natural "worship language," and give it daily priority. The more often we see how magnificent He is, the less we will be tempted to inflate the importance of other things.

Hope: Someday, we will forsake our idols, once and for all. That will be Heaven, literally. In that place, every thought, word, and action will point toward Him. That's actually what makes it Heaven…not the trappings that we typically focus on. Here's what I mean: When we talk about Heaven, we often tend to worry about whether or not our favorite things will be there.

"Will I be able to play golf in Heaven?"

"I heard there will be no death in Heaven. Does that mean I won't be able to go hunting anymore? Does that mean we won't eat meat?"

"I asked my pastor if my pets will be in Heaven, and he said he didn't know. If my pets won't be there, I'm not sure I want to go."

I think those are valid questions, and there are biblical ways to address them (although this book isn't the place).[xxiii] But if we fixate on them, we miss the ultimate point. Jesus will be there, and He will be enough. How do I know this? Because He created everything we love most about life: Fun, laughter, affection, good food, adventure, excitement. When we get to Heaven, we will bypass the middle-man and go straight to the source of all those things. How do I know that Jesus will be enough? Because when He came here in the flesh, people walked for days to see Him, then stood in the sun for hours to hear Him. He was magnetic. And we will have unhindered access to Him in that place. How do I know He will be enough? Because He is the most powerful being in the universe, who knows exactly what would be most likely to result in our happiness and flourishing, and He loves us enough to die for us, literally. I'm not great at math, but even I know that adds up to an eternal life that will put our greatest experiences on this earth to shame. And that's my point. Whether the things we enjoyed in this life will be there or not, I can't say for sure. But I know Jesus well enough to say this for sure: We won't be able to find a single fault with the world He has made for us. Whatever our expectations are, He will outstrip them.

Someday, we will see that Jesus is more than enough. I believe this is why we're commanded in Colossians 3:1-2,

If then you have been raised with Christ, seek the things that are above, where Christ is, seated at the right hand of God. Set your minds on things that are above, not on things that are on earth.

I take that verse literally. In fact, I think daydreaming about Heaven is one of the most productive ways we can spend our time. When we set our minds on the things above, we experience hope. And hope steals the power from our idols. If I know that someday, I will have everything I could ever want and more, I am less tempted to be greedy for earthly things. When I think about how every person I know will spend eternity somewhere, I focus less on my own temporary comfort and more on loving the people who God has placed in my life. And because I know that someday, I will bask in the unconditional love of my perfect Father, I feel foolish for worrying about the fleeting, fickle approval of people down here. When I live in hope, my idols seem as uninviting as a bag of stale Doritos at 10:30 on Thanksgiving morning. Sure, I'm hungry, and dinner's not ready yet. But I know it's coming. I can smell how good it's going to be. Why would I waste my time on tasteless corn triangles coated in chemically-modified cheese-flavored dust, when I have a feast prepared for me?

I will say it again: Someday, we will see that Jesus is more than enough. We'll know then that He always has been. And we'll wonder why we ever tried to find joy, peace, purpose and identity in anything else. So why not pursue an idol-free life right now? Not only could you and I live forever free, but we could be the start of a movement, as God's people finally shed their idols and return to Him with all their hearts. We often talk about a need for revival in America. We pray 2 Chronicles 7:14, as if God's promise to "heal our land" means that He'll overthrow the forces of secularism and put Christians on top of the pyramid. But that's not what that verse means, and that's not what revival is. In 2 Chronicles, God was promising Solomon that, even if

His people turn away from Him, He'll take them back if they only repent. That promise is still true. Revival is when redeemed people return to living with Jesus as their one true King, rejecting all the other false contenders who've been getting in the way. That is what our world needs to see. And by God's grace, it will happen. We'll live forever free.

NOTES

[i] https://www.guttmacher.org/fact-sheet/american-teens-sexual-and-reproductive-health

[ii] https://www.baptistpress.com/resource-library/news/two-thirds-of-teens-who-had-sex-wish-they-had-waited/

[iii] https://www.businessinsider.com/there-are-42-million-prostitutes-in-the-world-and-heres-where-they-live-2012

[iv] https://www.psychologytoday.com/us/blog/experimentations/201802/when-is-porn-use-problem

[v] https://www.rainn.org/statistics/scope-problem

[vi] https://comeawake.org/2017/06/01/the-idol-of-comfort/

[vii] Jen Michel Pollock, "Glennon Doyle Melton's Gospel of Self Fulfillment," Christianity Today, Nov 20, 2016.

[viii] In 930 BC, the nation of Israel was split in two. The ten Northern tribes made their capital in Samaria and continued to call themselves Israel, while the two Southern tribes (Judah and Benjamin) stayed in Jerusalem, led by the sons of David, and called themselves Judah. This is found in 1 Kings 12 and 2 Chronicles 10.

[ix] We think of Isaiah 7:14 as a Christmas verse, and for good reason. Matthew 1:23 says that Isaiah was predicting the virgin birth of Jesus. But it also referred to a young woman in Isaiah's time, whose pregnancy would be a ticking clock that told Ahaz how long he needed to wait for God's deliverance. It's common for prophecies to have a dual fulfillment: One that would occur in the prophet's own lifetime, and another, greater fulfillment in the distant future.

[x] "Clinton's Sins Aren't Private," Franklin Graham, *The Wall Street Journal*, August 27, 1998.

[xi] "What Kind of God is This?" Nancy LeTourneau, Washington Monthly, May 7, 2018.

[xii] https://www.christianitytoday.com/ct/2019/december-web-only/trump-should-be-removed-from-office.html

[xiii] https://www.politico.com/magazine/story/2018/01/23/tony-perkins-evangelicals-donald-trump-stormy-daniels-216498/

[xiv] If you're interested in the legal particulars, the two cases are McDougal v. Fox and Herring Networks, Inc v. Rachel Maddow, et al.

[xv] https://www.barna.com/research/racial-divides-spiritual-practice/

[xvi] Lawrence B. Finer, Lori F. Frohwirth, Lindsay A. Dauphinee, Susheela Singh and Ann M. Moore, "Reasons U.S. Women Have Abortions: Quantitative and Qualitative Perspectives," The Guttmacher Institute.

[xvii] David French, "In a Post-Roe World, Pro-Lifers Would Still Have a Lot of Work to Do." *National Review*, July 19, 2019.

[xviii] Daniel Silliman, "Promise Keepers Tried to End Racism 25 Years Ago. It Almost Worked." *Christianity Today*, June 21, 2021.

[xix] "The Demographics of Racial Inequality in the United States," Brookings, July 27, 2020.
[xx] Pew Research Center, "Attitudes on Same-Sex Marriage," May 14, 2019.
[xxi] https://www.prri.org/research/americas-growing-support-for-transgender-rights/

[xxii] *Are conservatives more charitable than liberals in the U.S.? A meta-analysis of political ideology and charitable giving,* sciencedirect.com.

[xxiii] I highly recommend Randy Alcorn's book, *Heaven: A Comprehensive Guide to Everything the Bible Says About Our Eternal Home.*

Made in the USA
Monee, IL
06 November 2023